What People Are Saying About
the *Teen Ink*™ Series . . .

"Real issues and real voices . . . This awesome collection of stories and poems will inspire readers."

BarnesandNoble.com

"What I read in these pages is lifesaving stuff. Not only is much of it astonishingly good from a craft point of view, but it gives teenagers *voice*. In a culture where adolescents are often ignored or treated as second-class citizens, *Teen Ink* gives them a place to say loud and clear who they are."

Chris Crutcher
author, *Staying Fat for Sarah Byrnes* and *Whale Talk*

"This book is a celebration of how honest, brilliant and passionate teenage voices are. All teens will thoroughly enjoy and relate to this book."

Kim Kirberger
author, *Chicken Soup for the Teenage Soul* series

"*Teen Ink* is about the trying times of teenage life. It's all about the joys and sorrows that teens go through on a daily basis. This book is about us—teenagers! These are our stories, our poems, our lives."

Charles "Chip" Pinder, age 17

"No adult reader can remain untouched by the drama in teens' lives; their writings provoke our compassion and insight. Teens themselves will savor every word from compatriots who so eloquently tell the truth."

Cathi Dunn MacRae
editor, *Voices of Youth Advocates*

"*Teen Ink* is like an open door to the hearts and souls of today's teens."

Melissa Gustafson, age 16

"*Teen Ink* is a forum for teens that the entire family can enjoy, learn from and use to communicate real emotions among themselves."

Chevy Chase
actor

"Teens writing for teens about teen stuff—what could be more compelling?"

Amazon.com

"*Teen Ink* is like a teenager's bible to life. Every page is another life lesson to help them grow and mature into young adults."

Lauren Kuller, age 16

"*Teen Ink* brings out the best in America's youth. They speak unapologetic truths from their hearts."

Rev. Jesse Jackson
civil-rights leader

"*Teen Ink* is the only book for us, by us. All others fail in comparison. This is the only book I have ever read that I truly relate to."

Geoff Richardson, age 17

"Their intensity and passion ring resoundingly from each poetry, fiction and nonfiction segment. Each piece is clear and lively, and the mix is varied. The black-and-white photographs and artwork express creative experimentation, which adds to the stark, candid voices of the young authors."

School Library Journal

"Every teen I know has been in a relationship, and it's wonderful to know that we aren't the only teens going through this stuff."

Kamilla Hassan, age 16

"It's thrilling to me to read these pieces by teen writers—not only because of the dozens and dozens of new ideas—but because of the *passion* for writing these teens bring to their work."

R. L. Stine
author, *Goosebumps, Fear Street* and
Nightmare Room series

"*Teen Ink* is the only book I've ever heard of that is for teens and written by teens. It can make you cry and make you laugh all within the same story."

Maggie Kelly, age 17

"These eloquent writings offer insight into the challenges, losses and changes of teenagers' lives. *Teen Ink* can help us all gain a better understanding of young people."

Alvin F. Poussaint, M.D.
professor of psychiatry, Harvard Medical School

"The stories in *Teen Ink* surely cannot be read only once; the advice they give, support they offer and real-life situations they provide allow the reader to know that he/she is not alone, and the reader is indefinitely connected to all the authors in this intimate literary wonder."

Danielle Scovel, age 16

"Teens looking for more substantial fare than music videos, mall sales and fashion magazines should check out *Teen Ink*. Adults, too, will gain insight into adolescent concerns."

U.S. Airways *Attaché* magazine

"I always find myself holding my breath at one point in each story, feeling the same anxiety and will to go on as the writer. *Teen Ink* truly takes me to another world and helps me look at life in a new light."

Emily Chase, age 13

"I am especially impressed when a book can fully engage my teenage son and compete so successfully with his beloved computer games."

Victoria Sutherland
publisher, *ForeWord*

"This book is an original, honest and refreshingly un-cheesy approach to 'keeping it real.' Teenagers are infinitely more savvy, insightful, sensitive and talented than given credit for."

Teenreads.com

"*Teen Ink* is a very inspirational book. It leaves me thinking and always helps me through the rough times."

Desirée Swanson, age 16

"*Teen Ink* invites young authors to write down and share their ideas, beliefs, feelings and aspirations."

Howard Gardner
author and educator, Harvard University

"An extremely entertaining book with many lessons, laughs and occasional saddness. This book will touch each person who reads it."

Peyton Jones, age 13

"*Love and Relationships* has the touch of a mother's hand. It guides you through a relationship, its good times, its bad ones and gives honest advice on how to lose and love again."

Audrey Bowlin, age 16

"Not only does this book touch my heart, it has the potential to inspire and comfort kids all over the world. These stories relate to teens' lives and help them realize they're not alone."

Jake Takiff, age 13

"*Teen Ink* is not only touching; it teaches me a different lesson on each page."

Cristina Buccellati, age 13

Edited by

Stephanie H. Meyer
John Meyer

Health Communications, Inc.
Deerfield Beach, Florida

www.hcibooks.com
www.TeenInk.com

The following pieces were originally published by The Young Authors Foundation, Inc. (©1989–2002) in *The 21st Century/Teen Ink* magazine. We gratefully acknowledge the many individuals who granted us permission to reprint the cited material.

"Couple on a Bench." Reprinted by permission of Sara Booth. ©2001 Sara Booth.

"His Name Was Jack." Reprinted by permission of Emily J. Copeman. ©2001 Emily J. Copeman.

(continued on page 332)

Library of Congress Cataloging-in-Publication Data

Teen ink : love and relationships / edited by Stephanie H. Meyer and John Meyer.

    p.   cm.

    Summary: A collection of stories and poems by teenage writers arranged in such categories as "Love Stories," "Ideal Portraits," "Everyday Happenings," "Bits of Memory," and "Different Connections."

    ISBN-10: 1-55874-969-1

    ISBN-13: 978-1-55874-969-6

    1. Adolescence—Literary collections.   2. Youth's writings, American. [1. Adolescence—Literary collections.   2. Youth's writings.] I. Meyer, Stephanie H., date. II. Meyer, John, date.

PZ5 .T29496 2002
810.8'09283—dc21

2002019986

Publisher: Health Communications, Inc.
    3201 S.W. 15th Street
    Deerfield Beach, FL 33442-8190

R-10-02

Cover illustration and design by Larissa Hise Henoch
Inside book design by Lawna Patterson Oldfield
Inside book formatting by Dawn Grove

"Love is the only sane and satisfactory answer to the problem of human existence."

—ERICH FROMM

"We must all live together as brothers or perish alone as fools."

—DR. MARTIN LUTHER KING, JR.

To all of those we love,
thank you

Contents

3. Challenging Tales

4. Ideal Portraits

5. Family Events

6. Monumental Moments

7. Everyday Happenings

Foreword

by R. L. Stine

"Where do you get your ideas?"

I spend a lot of time talking with young writers, and that is always the first question they ask me.

It's a very hard question to answer. Where *do* story ideas come from?

Sometimes I make a joke and tell them, "I get my ideas at the Idea Store." Of course, this is silly. But after a while, I started thinking: What if there really *was* an Idea Store?

What departments would you find in an Idea Store?

I think you'd find *three* departments—three places where story ideas come from. *One* would be the *Experience* Department. It contains everything you see and everything you do.

Two would be the *Memory* Department. It has everything you remember. The *third* department I call the *What If* Department. It contains everything you wonder about, everything you dream up and imagine . . . everything that makes you ask, "What if . . . ?"

I think all story ideas come from these three places. And as you will see, the wonderful stories, essays and poems collected in this book draw their inspiration from all three.

In "His Name Was Jack," Emily Copeman visits the Memory Department and remembers a romantic summer in which she met Jack, who changed her life.

Amilcar Silva, in "Sins of the Father," uses a horrifying experience—watching his father stab a man to death. Amilcar starts with that terrifying event and then describes how it shaped his attitudes toward his family.

Suzanne Timmons also visits the Experience Department in "Emily the Soccer Star." It's a touching portrait of a girl she met while working as a volunteer at a hospital.

Daniel Bailey begins his poem, "A Turtle-Shaped Box," in the What If Department. The poem starts with a dream in which he pulls his heart from his chest.

Yuck. If Daniel doesn't make it as a poet, he just might make a good horror writer!

It's thrilling to me to read these pieces by teen writers—not only because of the dozens and dozens of new ideas—but because of the *passion* for writing these teens bring to their work.

I found that passion when I was nine years old. That's when I started writing—and it changed my life. I hope that some of these teen writers will find the joy and success I have found. I know that you will be touched and amused and amazed by the writing collected here.

And, by the way, where do you get *your* ideas?

R. L. Stine has sold more children's books than anyone ever: 350,000,000! He has written too many books to mention, including the Goosebumps, Fear Street *and* Nightmare Room *series.*

Preface

by Shea M. Seen

Being a teenager isn't easy. It seems like you have a million thoughts, ideas and emotions rushing through your body every second, but they're moving so fast, you just can't seem to grab one and make sense of it, let alone get it out. And even if you do manage to blurt out a thought or come to some conclusion about one of your ideas, no one wants to listen to you. You're a teenager. You live in what my stepdad calls "The Dark Side." What do you know anyway?

And so, as teenagers, we often feel as though we've been left alone. No one listens to us; no one understands us; we don't even understand ourselves.

But even if we're often not sure what to say or think, we have to get our feelings out somehow and, for many of us, the only way to do that is through writing. We begin telling our problems and secrets to a diary, write stories about ourselves where we name the main character Shelly instead of Kelly, try to express ourselves through poetry and compose music.

But even that isn't as easy as it sounds.

Writing is this funny thing. I mean, you have all these memories in your head, and yet, somehow getting them out, finding the words to express them and writing them so they adequately express the picture you have in your head, seems so much more difficult.

"I remember sitting under this tree," you start, "this *shady* tree," "under this tree that was blowing in the breeze," "a *cool* breeze," "a *breezy* breeze"? You let out a sigh and throw down your pen.

You know what *you're* trying to say. So, what's up with your pen?!

I consider myself a writer, but I've felt this way a million times, trying to describe how I felt my first day of school, or looking out over the mountains of presents my first Christmas, the rush I got the first time I was on stage, or the first time I saw the ocean.

As I got older, I tried to describe my first crush, my first kiss, my first time falling in love, and eventually, the first time my heart got broken. When you enter your teenage years, it seems that your focus changes slightly from the world around you to the world of the opposite sex.

All of us have memories like these, of good times, sad times, times spent with that special someone and first times. Those special moments will live in our hearts and minds forever.

And that's what makes these *Teen Ink* books so great—they're written by teens just like you or me. Teens who have moments just like yours or mine. By those who actually got their feelings and memories down on paper so all of us could benefit. Those who were willing to share their experiences with us so that we could better understand ourselves and each other.

Finally, teenagers have an outlet to express their thoughts and ideas. And the rest of us have a place to go and relate to others our age, who are going through the same things we are and know how we feel.

Finally, someone is listening.

As you flip through these pages, you'll find yourself laughing out loud, ooohing and awwwing, thinking, *I know exactly how you feel,* or *I wish I would have said that!*

And maybe you'll find a little bit of your story in here, too.

It's there, trust me.

Because in reality, we all share the same story. It's called life.

Shea M. Seen, still a teen, also wrote the amusing remembrance, "Here Comes the Bride," on page 238.

Introduction

Welcome to our fourth book in the *Teen Ink* series. We can't believe that in the short span of two years we've put together four books filled with the creativity of teens. Actually, it's been exciting, since we've had over 25,000 pieces to choose from that have appeared in our monthly magazine, *Teen Ink*. And that's exactly what we did to create these collections: re-read all the pieces we've published and selected some of the most astounding.

You see, for thirteen years now, teens across America have been sending us their hopes, dreams and fears in poems, prose and artwork. And we've given them a forum each month to showcase these amazing tales. More than 350,000 submissions have come to us over the years. We've never had staff writers or assigned stories, so every piece comes from their hearts. We've also been astounded by the dramatic reactions of other teens who've sent thousands of their letters and feedback that document how they, too, know just how Lisa felt when she went on her first date, or when Kevin lost his father. They, too, had been there, but never realized there were others out there who felt the same way.

And isn't connecting what it's all about, really? Here is the latest collection of these voices in a volume filled with tales of love and relationships. What is more important than how we all relate, connect and sometimes disconnect? What is closer to the hearts of teens everywhere than their loves and relationships? Of course, there are relationships of all types: between friends, teacher and student, with that stranger, with family and, of course, the relationship that is the beginning of that all-important joining of couples. They express their thoughts with, at times, humor, pathos and beauty, but always with a candor which captures that special moment when it finally all makes sense.

Although this is the fourth collection, and the voices change in each volume, much does remain constant. Like the other books, every word you find in *Teen Ink: Love and Relationships* is written by teens. After we selected far too many of our favorites, we asked 4,000 teenagers in junior- and senior-high schools across the country to read sample chapters and tell us which pieces they liked best. And, just like with the other books, all royalties are donated directly to the nonprofit Young Authors Foundation to offer opportunities for teenagers to express themselves.

You, the reader, will find amazing candor, emotion and insight expressed by these teenagers. So, flip through these pages and sample these amazing pieces. You will be compelled to continue reading to discover more of the depth and sensitivity of these teens whose views of love and relationships surely parallel our own.

Stephanie H. Meyer
John Meyer

Welcome

This is your book! All the words and images on these pages were created by teens just like you and gathered from pieces that appeared in *Teen Ink* magazine during the past twelve years.

Did you know that this is the fourth book in the *Teen Ink* series? The first three (*Teen Ink: Our Voices, Our Visions; Teen Ink 2: More Voices, More Visions* and *Teen Ink: Friends and Family*) are all available in bookstores nationwide and on the Web.

You can join these teenagers by sending us *your* stories, poems, art and photography to be considered for the monthly *Teen Ink* magazine and future books in this series.

If you want to participate, see the submission guidelines on page 299. You can send your submissions through our Web site: *www.TeenInk.com,* e-mail us at *editor@TeenInk.com* or through the mail to Teen Ink, Box 97, Newton, MA 02461.

To learn more about the magazine and to request a free sample copy, see our Web site at *www.TeenInk.com.*

Love Stories

Photo by Sara Booth

His Name Was Jack

by Emily J. Copeman

It was about 8:00 P.M. on a Saturday in April. I was standing on the floor of the gymnasium at the high school surrounded by hundreds of students, my eardrums quivering from the music blasting from gigantic speakers. I felt slightly nauseated by the blur of people whirling around me, and my face was flushed.

A thick coat of concealer covered the dark circles under my eyes, the result of a long week of rehearsals for the school musical and lack of sleep. I followed my best friend through the crowd of unfamiliar faces, allowing myself to be hauled through the masses of teenage boys who smelled as if they had bathed in cologne.

As we finally reached our friends, a slow song began. I watched with amusement as my classmates darted frantically through the crowd, searching for someone to dance with, when my gaze met a pair of piercing brown eyes.

A boy a few inches taller than I approached and asked me to dance. I nodded and put my arms around his neck, studying the faces of my friends as they inspected him. After receiving the thumbs-up from my friends, I learned his name was Jack; he was a student there. As we talked

I noticed he frequently laughed, and when he did, his eyes twinkled.

For the rest of the evening I danced only with Jack, sometimes asking questions, other times just resting my head on his shoulder, feeling surprisingly comfortable. At the end of the night he thanked me for a fun time and disappeared into the crowd. My friends surrounded me almost instantly, asking about this handsome boy.

The rest of the weekend I wondered about the mysterious stranger. Monday I returned to the monotonous life at my all-girls school. All week I was enveloped in preparations for the upcoming musical and my memories of that dance faded.

After a hectic weekend of two exciting performances, I found myself home before dinner on Monday—a rare occurrence. As I lay sprawled on my bed, attempting to solve a geometry equation, my mother knocked on the door and handed me the phone, whispering, "It's a boy, but no one I know."

I took a deep breath and murmured, "Hello?" An unexpectedly deep voice responded, "Hi, this is Jack, from the dance. Chris gave me your number."

Moments later we were talking like old friends. Although the conversation was short, I knew it would be the first of many. Jack and I spoke on the phone every night, although our schedules made it difficult to see each other. He asked me to his semi-formal and I agreed to go if he would come to mine.

May rolled around quickly, and I discovered he was the perfect date at my dance. Meeting my parents, Jack was outgoing and friendly. He had handpicked my corsage, which fit perfectly and matched my dress. By the end of the evening, I was entranced by Jack's smile and charming personality.

For his dance, he wore a pale blue suit from a vintage shop and a tie that matched my dress. When we arrived, I noticed he was the only guy who had strayed from the generic dark dress pants and white shirt. He was proud of his suit and comfortable being different; he laughed when anyone pointed out that he looked silly. He introduced me to his friends and insisted on dancing and singing to every song. By the end of the night, I'd agreed to be his girlfriend and was glowing with pride and affection.

Long school days and final exams came to an end and the warm, sunny days of summer arrived. Every night I looked forward to the ring of the telephone at 8:30 and the sound of his upbeat voice saying, "Hi! How was your day?" We grew close very quickly, always having a wonderful time whether we went to dinner and a movie or had a skeeball competition at the local arcade.

The beginning of June I realized I loved him. Each morning, when the rays of sunshine streamed into my room, I opened my eyes to the promise of a new day that would be wonderful because I was loved. Even when I felt unappreciated after a long, tiring day at work, the thought of Jack's beautiful eyes glowing with earnest compassion and love reminded me that life was wonderful.

Although I knew I liked Jack for his kind, honest charm and handsome appearance, I wasn't immediately sure why I liked him more than other boys. He wasn't the smartest or the best athlete, but over the summer I came to understand why I adored him.

I had lived the first two years of high school as if they were a great punishment. I felt that every day was a waste of my time, and everyone frustrated me because they didn't understand my thoughts and feelings. I loathed the behavior of my peers and felt I had nothing to offer the world. I felt dissatisfied following the rules. I wanted to defy convention and try things I had been taught never to do.

When I met Jack, I was amazed at what a happy person he was, eager to do and try everything, accepting challenges with an energy and excitement for life. He always searched for the good in everyone and the positive in every situation. He loved soccer, and always played as hard as he could, determined to do his best and offer his all to the team. Even after losing, he shook his opponents' hands with an earnest respect.

Jack never tried to be like anyone else, never chose clothes that would help him blend in with the crowd, and was always content to be recognized as an individual. He had friends from different groups and grades, and was known as both a leader (having been elected repeatedly to Student Council) and a friend.

When I look back on the summer, I am flooded with a warm nostalgia for the days I spent with Jack biking to the beach, walking hand-in-hand, diving off rocks and enjoying picnic dinners. After nine months, when I get ready for an evening with him, butterflies still dance in my stomach!

Every day since that first April night has been a step on

a long journey within myself. I have learned the value of living life to the fullest, and I have grown to accept myself and others for what we have to offer. I realize I am still young and naive, but I know I am blessed to have already met my soul mate and best friend. ▣

On the Bus

by Shana Onigman

If this bus ka-thunks over one more bump in the road I swear I'll scream. If it weren't for this ka-thunking, I could just squeeze my eyes shut and pretend I'm not even moving. Wheels aren't rolling. Bus isn't going. I'm not even on a bus. I'm curled up by myself in my own little world where no one can reach me, where I don't have to be. . . . There, it ka-thunked again. Darn bus. This is ridiculous. Why am I scared? Why am I doing this? Why don't I just stand up and scream at the bus driver, "Turn the bus around. Go back! I've changed my mind. I don't want to go. Take me home!" Of course, he wouldn't listen to me. I could hijack this bus and send it back home, then get off and run home. I'd be safe at home in an hour.

It's okay. It's okay. I've planned this for weeks. I know what I'm doing. I've gone over all the details a trillion times. All I can say is, that kid better be there when I get off this bus. If he isn't, I'll never believe anyone again. I thought I'd believe him to the end of the world. No, if he's a liar I won't even believe one word anyone ever says. I'll just assume everyone's lying. But how could he lie to me? We've been writing letters for how long now? A year? Is that all? And I don't even know what he looks like or what he sounds like, for Pete's sake. I haven't a clue. I just have a box full of letters, a bus ticket and all the brainless impulsiveness of a lovesick sixteen-year-old. . . . Wait, what's that? I can't be in love with the kid; I've never met him! What if he hates me? What if I'm nothing like my letters—or he's nothing like his and I've been wrong all along?

I get a postcard that says, "Come visit me on the 10th" and I'm off on a bus at quarter of seven in the morning. Where's my reason? Logic? I used to be logical in math class; I was logical. Now I can't even figure out if I have enough money for the ticket home . . . home . . . home is so far away. I've never been this far from home by myself and I'm so scared.

Oh, don't cry. No, no, please God. Don't let me cry now; don't reduce me to nothing but a helpless baby. He can't see that I've been crying. If he ever even sees me at all, if he even finds me. There must be forty people on this bus. What if he walks up to that pretty girl in front of me, that gorgeous blonde, and says, "Hi, it's me"? What will I do? "Sorry, it's me you're looking for, my regrets." And how will I know it's him, anyway? Maybe it's a big practical joke, a year-long practical joke, ha ha, and he's the most incredible liar and I'm the most gullible fool who ever walked the face of this enormous, ENOR-MOUS planet. . . . Can't I stop these childish tears, for once? Oh, if this bus ka-thunks again I swear I'll . . .

Is this it? That's the station, right there. Yes, the bus is slowing down . . . we're here. Omigod, omigod, omigod, I'm here, I'm here and somewhere in that station he's waiting, he's waiting for me and only m—omigod! My name? Big brown cardboard sign with my name on it, and IT'S IN HIS WRITING . . . here he is. That's him. So this is how he'd know he'd find me. And I have to go up to him and say, "Hi, it's me . . . it's me, I'm here, I'm absolutely insane but I think I'm in love with you" . . . , and I think I can do it. ▣

Photo by Matt Bullock

Valentine's Day

by Amanda R. Grier

They were beautiful flowers. I couldn't argue that. There were twelve red roses with baby's breath as their companions. But their smell was mundane, store-bought and predictable.

The sky was one big gray cloud, limitless and unending. I set the deep red carnations I had given him on the dashboard of his car. I couldn't help but notice the red of the carnations riding toward the gray of the sky.

My stomach turned.

"Here, I bought you some chocolates." He reached behind him and pulled out a red heart-shaped box.

"Thanks," I accepted it nervously. Was I supposed to kiss him now? I didn't. The chocolates and the flowers were romantic, but . . .

The high grass brushed my summer legs as he carried me on his back. The breeze reached its fingers toward my hair. I ran my hand through my hair as if imitating this unseen force. The sky looked as if I were staring into the depths of the ocean, instead of the expanse of the heavens. His cheek felt soft against mine, almost babylike.

"Wait." Letting me slide gently down his back, he got on his knees. Straining to see over his shoulder, I saw him digging softly through a patch of weeds.

"What are you doing?" I playfully asked. Facing me, he held up a delicate little flower. The colors in this little piece of art dazzled me. It was almost blue and not quite purple. Holding the tiny gift in his massive hands, he reached for the blue clay jar that hung from a cord around my neck. He held the bottom of the jar with the tips of his fingers and placed the gift into the empty hole.

He looked at me with his intense ocean-blue eyes and gave me that boyish grin that never turned into a smile unless I approved.

"Now, your jar won't be empty anymore."

I lost that flower a while ago, and I lost those eyes, and now the little blue jar hangs around my neck . . . empty. ▣

Back to Life

by George L. Newton III

I never knew what life was until she came. My words pushed people away. My days were spent talking of life as if it were some dead thing that interested me in only the most abstract way. I was just a shell filled with what others said. A sheep they could lead anywhere they wanted.

I filled my head with lies. I could make myself believe, "I'm not lonely. I don't need love." She saw through my lies. I resisted as her hands tried to pull me back into life. I was incapable of love. I would just hurt her. Her lips kept asking, but I couldn't understand. "No" was the only word I knew. She kept asking.

The first week I looked at myself. What did she see? My eyes were their same dull color. My hair went in as many different directions as it always had. I could still hear her words. Why did she love me? My heart jumped. I wanted to know. Her face lost all color when I finally said, "Yes."

As I sat in the back row with my arm around her (a move copied from some half-remembered movie), I could suddenly see what the couple on the screen were seeing in each other's eyes. I can still remember the moment when we said our good-byes. The soft glow from the porch light. The way our lips fumbled together. Her eyes as they sparkled while she gradually drifted away. I would sell my soul to live this moment again. Her soft giggle as her dad's voice called her inside will always haunt me.

The world that greeted me the next day wasn't the same one I'd lived in for seventeen years. Something had changed as I danced home. The world was softer. Safer. She taught me to listen. I could feel what I had tried to ignore my whole life. For the first time, I could talk of myself. My mind started racing. If she could care so deeply for me, what about others? My family. My friends. I began to give back the love I felt. I caught myself smiling the other day. I'll probably try it again.

Before, I thought of love as some dead thing that could never affect me. My words would protect me. She helped topple my house of lies. I know what love is. I can understand what life is. She taught me more than any book ever could. I know who I am. I never knew what life was until I met her. ◙

Sean's Visit

by Liz Antle

He didn't ring the doorbell—he never did—but somehow I always knew he was there. Sean sat on my front porch, hunched over with his back to the door. His bleached-blond buzz cut was growing back and sticking out on all sides.

I looked at him through the glass door, debating whether or not I should open it this time. He was always asking for more than I could give. I slowly opened the door, and without turning around he asked, "You got time?"

Perhaps tonight he just wanted to talk.

"Yeah," I whispered as I sat down next to him. "What's wrong?" I looked over and realized his eyes were red and swollen. Every once in a while his lip would quiver, and his hands shook as he hurriedly took another drag of his cigarette.

"Nothing new," he said as smoke filtered out of his mouth. "Wanna see something?"

"I don't know, do I?" I asked hesitantly. He rolled up the left leg of his oversized khakis and revealed his pain. The wound, starting to scab over, had stained the inside of his pants.

"I jumped out of my window to be with you."

"Really?" I asked sarcastically. I could smell the whiskey on his breath and knew something had gone terribly wrong.

"Naw, more to get away from him."

Sean's dad was an alcoholic, some days more than others.

"They had another fight," he mumbled under his cigarette. "About me. Jerry's a real jerk sometimes, and Dad knows how mad he makes me." I sat in silence, listening. Sometimes I felt more like a psychiatrist than a friend. He had been my best friend all my life.

I remember one time his father took us down to the park to go snake hunting. My mother thought it would be a well-supervised trip, but Sean's father took off our invisible leashes and left us to roam.

Sean's goal in life was to scare me. He always said I was the biggest tomboy he knew, and that one day he would bring out the girl in me. While walking through the forest, he began telling me about the most dangerous snake in Connecticut: the red-tailed cobra. All of a sudden he shouted, "There it is, there it is, run for your life!" Like a gullible little girl, I ran away crying. He told me later he was kidding, but it took me almost a day to recover. Ever since, Sean treated me differently. It was as if that day marked the beginning of something more than friendship. It was the first day he saw me as more than just one of the guys.

"I came home wasted last night. . . ." How quickly things were changing. He knew I couldn't let it happen again.

"Don't look at me like that," he demanded.

"Like what?"

"Like you hate me. It was a party and one thing led to another—but it doesn't matter."

"You smell like it today."

"Like what?"

"Like whiskey."

He just sat there looking at me. I turned away until he finally said, "When I woke up this morning, they had locked me in my room. I know it was Jerry's idea because my dad doesn't care about, well, anything."

"That's not true."

"It is, you know it is. I woke up and there was a note on my door saying, 'You're grounded.' You're grounded, that's it! So I sat in my room, just staring at the wall until it finally got dark, and I jumped out my window. So that's why I'm here."

"You're here because you're grounded?"

"Yeah, I guess so. Mostly because I need your help. Dad says if I don't get my act together, Mom won't send Theresa down."

Theresa was his sister. He loved her more than anything in the whole world. More than cigarettes, he once told me.

"So what can I do?"

"You can help me get better. Will you?" I couldn't believe what he was asking. Help him get better? Every day Sean would tell me how he was going to give up cigarettes or stop drinking. Some days he would even promise never to bleach his hair again, like that mattered! But help him get better?

"Better from what?"

"Better, you know, better. I want to stop drinking, smoking, jumping out of windows, begging for your help . . . failing."

"Failing? What do you mean? In school? Because school doesn't matter."

"It does to my mom, so it does to me. If Mom's happy, so am I because then Theresa can come and I can stop worrying about her. If she's here, I can protect her." Sean was always trying to protect everyone: his sister, his mom, even me. He walked me to school every morning so the thugs wouldn't harass me. He held my hand as we walked through the metal detectors so the cops wouldn't take advantage of me. He was my bodyguard, and now? Now he was asking me to be his.

"Will you?" he pouted.

"Oh," I reached over and grabbed his hands, "fine."

He just laughed, a small, light chuckle that sent me into fits of laughter each time I heard it. His smile could fill an empty room, and it was with a smile that he looked best. He jumped off the porch, sat on the grass and fell back to look at the moon. I ran over and jumped on top of him.

"I've been thinking," he announced. "I've been thinking that you and I should run away together."

"Oh, okay."

"No, seriously, we need to run away."

"Maybe." But he knew I never would. Sean looked up and smiled his big, toothy smile.

"I love you," he whispered into the sky. "I love you so much," he said now looking at me. I just laughed, I don't know why, but it seemed funny at the time. He stood up, offered me a hand, but instead picked me up over his shoulder. He ran up and down the street, laughing and making fun of my screaming, until we fell down on the cold grass.

My mom signaled from the window it was time to come in. Sean saw me looking at her, turned to the window and waved hello. He had always loved my mother. I motioned I'd be there soon.

Sean and I both turned around in unison. It was like a movie. His life was the tragic obstacle the main character had to overcome. He was determined that this movie was going to have a happy ending.

"Now, my lady," he said as he helped me off the ground, "we must say good night." I turned to him, saw his half smile and laughed. I laughed so hard, I broke into tears.

"What?" he asked through his own laughter. "What? What's so funny?"

Suddenly, his blue eyes caught mine, and I stopped. There was an awkward silence, which he quickly filled with a kiss. It was like a dream, but as quickly as it had come, it was gone and forgotten as he asked, "So, are you going to run away with me?" I just smiled. "I'm serious."

"Yeah, sure, just not tonight." Pretending to be mad, he blew smoke in my face, got up and left. When he was at the corner of my street, he turned and shouted, "Don't forget!" and, smiling, flicked his cigarette into the bush, glowing the whole way home. ▣

Sins of the Father

by Amilcar Silva

I am one of those kids who has lived my life without a father. He did not flee his family, but out of rage and jealousy, stabbed a man in front of my seven-year-old eyes, killing him. The image of my father with blood on his hands and tears in his eyes has remained with me my whole life. Charged with first-degree murder, he was deported to Cape Verde, and I've never seen him again. The day he was sent away my mother cried, not knowing how she would support my brother and me. Raising two boys was a heavy burden on her back. A strong, persevering woman, my mother took three jobs to support us. She hardly saw us because she never came home, going from one shift to another without rest.

I never had a father to teach me to be a man. My mother had to do that, too, and it is a good thing she did because in ninth grade I became a father myself. When I found out my girlfriend was pregnant, I was afraid life was over for me. I dreaded the thought of telling my mother, who already had so many burdens. When I did, she was very supportive and told me how to be a responsible father.

"You know what you need to do, right?" she said. "Get

a job and offer all your love and assistance to your girl-friend. Don't be like your father. Be a real man."

Since ninth grade I have tried to be the father and the man my mother believed I could be. I have worked two jobs so I can buy everything my baby needs—food, a crib and clothes. At the same time, I've stayed in school, even playing varsity football as a running back. I also became a peer mediator because I know that anger and violence can take a life and place a heavy burden on the family. I have mediated over one hundred conflicts during my four years in high school. Even though I struggle, I stay on top of my school work.

Most teenage fathers do not hang around, but I am going to stick like cement. I have no other choice but to be a part of my daughter's life, to support her, to provide for her and to give her nothing but love. People sometimes say that a mother is the most important parent in a child's life, but without a father, a child's life is not complete. My father made a decision not to be there for his boy, who is now a man and a proud father himself. Every child in the world has dreams, and most only wish for both parents to be a part of his or her life. My daughter does not have to worry about my leaving because I will never do anything to hurt her.

I will never forget the day my daughter was born. It was 9:00 P.M. when I received the phone call saying, "It's time." Because of the long hours of labor, my girlfriend's doctors decided to perform a Caesarean section. I was holding my girlfriend's hand when I heard a loud cry. I saw the doctor slowly lift out a little girl. When the doctor gave her to me, I said, "Hush, little baby. Daddy is here." She opened her eyes and looked at me, wrapped her tiny little hand around my finger and stopped crying. At that moment my heart melted, and I knew from her tight grip that we were going to be very close.

My daughter gives me strength every time I look into her eyes. If I feel down or lazy, all I have to do is picture how her life would be if I am not successful. My future is held in her tiny palms. I am determined to succeed. My daughter is my sun, moon and stars—my motivation and the love of my life. ◙

Art by William K. Sheppard

A Bookstore Romance

Fiction by Alice Reagan

I work in a bookstore, and my favorite section is Mystery. The women and men who buy these books are the ones you'd never suspect. Quiet, unassuming people with thick glasses and dark curly hair. They come in the store silently; they know what they want. They slide over to the back corner of the store, on the other side of Children's, and peruse their favorite author's shelf. Most mystery writers have a series, and the true connoisseur has read them all. The only reason they come to the store is to pick up the latest installment. And if it's only available in hardcover? No problem. These people are addicts, and they're not cheap. I've seen many a Sue Grafton junkie plunk down $22.50 for a novel that will be devoured in an hour and a half.

Mysteries feel great. They are all basically the same size, about an inch thick. I can fit five at one time in each hand. I love the way they slide into their places on the shelf, perfect every time. They have such great titles, too. *The Face of Death, Murder at the Monastery.*

I was straightening the Garden section, putting *Gardening the Easy Way* in front of *The Weekend Gardener,* when I saw him. He was an aisle over in the

Literature section, reading the back of *Madame Bovary*. His name was Matt. I recognized him from school; he had just graduated, and it was June. That night I would search the yearbook for his picture, pore over his senior quote, memorize his face. But just then, I knew it was lust. *May I help you?* I'd say, sauntering over to him, looking him straight in the eyes and almost startling him with my direct approach.

Why, yes, if you would, he'd reply. *I was just looking for a romance. Do you know any good ones?*

Ah, my specialty, I would purr. I was so very coy. Jane Eyre *is the best of the Gothic romances, but* Lady Chatterley's Lover *is also fabulous. . . .*

"Ellen? Ellen. Ellen!"

"Uh—what? God, you scared me to death." I awoke from my daydreaming to the acned face of Ron, my boss. Ick.

"The regional manager is going to be here within the hour. Can you move on to Social Sciences, please? This half of the store looks fine."

I grunted at Ron. He didn't deserve my attention. I looked around, but Matt had left.

The next day when I came into work, there was a note on the counter for me.

"Ellen—straighten—Psychology—call in special orders—vacuum—Thanks—Ron"

Ron didn't use punctuation. It was too committed. Ron also never called the Psychology section by its new name: Self-Help. I think Ron just wanted to show off that he knew how to spell psychology.

Self-Help took up a whole wall, behind Travel and

across from New Age. It was really a mess—some shelves were overstocked while others had wide white gaps. It was supposed to be alphabetical by subject, then within each subject, alphabetical by author. The subjects were all out of order, never mind the authors. I think it made some of my coworkers nervous to be around Self-Help. I know Ron avoided it completely: Self-Help was embarrassing. It was for vulnerable divorcées looking for a lover: *How to Marry the Man You Want NOW!* It was for those who couldn't control themselves: *It's Not What You're Eating, It's What's Eating YOU.* It was for . . . it was for Matt, who was browsing two shelves away from where I was crouched on the floor in a skirt, rearranging misplaced books and mumbling about how no one who shelved this section knew the alphabet.

Excuse me, Miss? He'd say earnestly, his cowlick standing his hair on end, his cheeks almost purple with embarrassment.

Yes? Can I help you in some way? I'd say graciously, rising—no, floating up to his eye level from where I had been shelving, my swanlike neck bowed gracefully. I was looking for a book called, um, *Overcoming Shyness.* (Matt was so adorable when he stammered.)

Why, I know that book, I'd say, quite sure of myself. *It's right here.* I ran my fingertips along the spines of the books until I came to it. Right there. And I would start to pull out the book for him when—Oh God, it was right next to *How to Satisfy a Woman Every Time and Have Her Begging for More!*

This was awful, just the most awkward, most mortifying thing that could ever . . .

"Ellen, are you doing anything or just staring at the sex books? Huh?"

"God, Ron, I am not staring at the sex books. I'm fixing this section, and if whoever put these away in the first place had done it right, I could be doing something else."

I looked around, but Matt had left.

The next time I worked, there was a huge shipment of New Fiction in, twenty boxes full. I love brand-new books, almost as much as I love Mystery. Brand-new books, heavy with important words, heavy with beautiful covers, dust jackets with raised letters, pages that smell like the world. I love the authors' pictures on the back covers. Authors look like real, live people. Most of them are kind of chunky around the middle. They almost always wear their favorite pair of jeans and an old shirt to the photo shoot; they look like the people across the street. I like the ones who smile best. It shows they don't take themselves too seriously.

Each book has to be checked in on an invoice. One mark next to the number of books received, another next to the price to make sure they match. I like checking in the books. It's exciting to pull out the latest novel by a famous author, to be the first one to see it, to hold it, to feel its exact weight and width in my hands. It's not exciting, though, when the sticker price is wrong on forty-five copies of the new Stephen King novel, and I have to split all my fingernails prying the price off and write up new ones to slap on the inside flap.

I was chewing on my lower lip—I do that when I'm aggravated—and carefully, carefully pulling off about the 300 millionth sticker, trying not to rip the dust jacket, and I was thinking about Matt. Maybe I could impress him by finding a really obscure book on the microfiche machine. . . .

You look kind of lost. Can I find something for you? I'd murmur in Matt's ear, as he was stumbling around the Dictionary section.

I really didn't think you would have it anyway. I was looking for a Yiddish-English dictionary for my grand-mother, kind of a surprise, but you don't seem—(he was so kind, so generous with his time, helping his bedridden grandmother like that).

Well, let me look it up on the fiche. Maybe I can order it.

Oh! You can do that? I had no idea. Wow. He'd look at me adoringly, with those beautiful blue eyes.

I'd stroll over to the fiche machine, push Ron aside and speedily find what Matt was looking for. *Ah, here's one I think your grandmother would love to have. . . .*

"Hey, Ellen, I didn't know you worked at this book-store. I come here all the time. What's up?"

I looked around. Matt was standing right there. ▣

The Phone Call

by Shannon P. Miller

A s she leaned over her nightstand to answer the phone, she glanced at the clock. Glaring back at her in bright red was the time—2:07 A.M. Who would call at two o'clock in the morning? She answered the phone with a very tired "hello." Her greeting was answered with another "hello" in that familiar voice. Immediately, she felt the comfortable warmth that always filled every part of her body when she heard his voice. She was still partially asleep and could not read the tone of his voice. Was he all right? Did he need help? He could sense her fear and reassured her that he was fine. He had come home late from his game and was trying unsuccessfully to fall asleep. He had been thinking about her and had something he needed to say.

What could it be? she thought as she listened intently to his breathing. It seemed heavy and deliberate. She waited. Silence, though this was different. It was comfortable and calm. It also seemed necessary. It was definitely not the uncomfortable silence she had experienced when talking to other guys. With him she did not feel she had to fill in the spaces of dead air with a stupid joke or the self-conscious giggle that can sometimes take over. She knew that he had something he wanted to say but was nervous. She would wait until he was ready. She was content to listen to his breathing for as long as it took. She could be waiting for him to tell her that he never wanted to see her again but for some reason she felt at that moment whatever he said would somehow be fine.

She did not want to push him into saying something he did not want to say so she reassuringly told him that he could tell her anything and he did not have to worry. He thanked her for being so patient. He finally stammered out, "I . . . think . . . um . . . I think that . . . well, it's just that I think I'm falling in love. . . ."

All of a sudden, the peacefulness she had known while listening to his breathing was interrupted, ". . . with you." What he said after that was muffled by her own disbelief that he was actually saying this. She knew that their relationship had been growing stronger over the past few months. She had thought that she might love him, but how was she supposed to know? Was she feeling love now, or was it just that she felt she had to express a love to validate his feelings? Was she ready to admit her love? Was it love? She felt as if her thoughts had been put in slow motion. Slowly, she could feel him slipping further away as his voice became increasingly distant. Is this what love does? Was it love that was now pulling them apart?

She could not hear him anymore. All she could hear was the persistent beeping of her alarm clock and the sound of her phone telling her it was off the hook. She could feel herself coming out of her sleep slowly and hesitantly, trying to hold onto the comfort that sleep brings. She felt as if she was searching to find the warmth his voice gave her and the admission of love that voice had spoken. She was fearing the worst and hoping for the best. As she awoke, she could feel the phone under her arm. There was a knot in her stomach and a lump in her throat. He had told her he was falling in love with her. How could it have been a dream when her emotions felt so real? Now all she could feel was the uncomfortable silence of her room as she started another day of longing to know his true feelings, where their hearts would lead them, and the words that would eventually be spoken originating from the feelings in their hearts. 🔲

Photo by Jon Wright

That Strange-Looking Boy

by Jenny Pirkle

The crowd wasn't very big, maybe thirty people, and no one was watching the tiny stage. I wandered closer, weaving between the little tables that struggled to support giant umbrellas, even though it was already dark and the black sky with its scattered crumbs of fire showed no signs of rain.

I don't know what lured me down to the front, unless it was the peculiar stare I felt bouncing from my lips to my eyes and back again from the strange-looking boy with a big nose sitting on the edge of the stage. He wore a jean jacket over a black T-shirt and baggy jeans. He had pale skin that looked almost yellow in the street lamps. His hair was so black it was almost blue, and it fell gracefully into the most amazing green eyes I had ever seen.

If his hair was graceful, I wasn't. I stumbled over the cobblestones, lost in our unspoken connection. When I looked up again, he was gone. A few more steps and I found him at the front of the platform, moving the milk can that served as a tip jar for the band, as if to say that he couldn't accept money for what he was about to do.

The last guitar note of the song died away as a boy whispered "thank you" into the microphone and smiled at the two or three people who clapped. He glanced at the strange-looking boy and gave a little nod. He nodded back almost imperceptibly and hopped onto the stage to join the guitar player/singer, saxophone player and drummer. Then the strange-looking boy took his violin from its case and began to rub something up and down the strings of the bow so tenderly that I couldn't help but wonder if he had some sort of unhealthy attachment to it.

I recognized the song at once; it was by Dave Matthews. The other three played well for teenagers, building to the point when I knew the violin would enter. It happened just as I thought; he came in perfectly, with a movement so natural it was as if he hadn't moved at all.

I am sure the other members of the band continued to play, just as I am sure people behind me didn't stop talking to enjoy it. I am positive that it was still nighttime in Savannah, Georgia, and I have no doubt that the strange-looking boy played for an audience of more than one. But the moment music sprang from beneath his chin, the band was silent, people were silent. The street was flooded with the brightest light.

And the boy was playing his violin for me.

And for himself. I soon realized that the light which had consumed the two of us radiated directly from his amazing green eyes, proof of the fiery passion that burned inside him. The light was a sphere that lifted us into the sky to unite with the stars and join the heavenly orchestra playing so fiercely that only their own ears could follow the spectral notes. His motions were so fluid that I could scarcely believe he actually coaxed the music from an instrument, imagining that he simply willed sounds to exist.

As for me, I had no instrument. I could only be, standing frozen in the flames of his talent.

And he played.

He played his violin, and it didn't matter that he was only a strange-looking boy. He played, and it didn't bother him that the milk can sat empty, hidden from view. He played and the street was made of gold and the stars over Savannah were his audience and his accompaniment. And when he looked at me again with a stare that bounced, I fell in love with him for proving to me that when you really enjoy living, big noses and empty milk cans don't matter.

Finally, when I once again felt the street beneath me, I looked for him, but he was gone. Another boy whispered "thank you" into the microphone and smiled at the two or three people who clapped. ▣

Love Sees No Colors

by Susan A. Eldred

I am scribbling this story on a worn-out notepad I found in my bag. The pages are unbelievably wrinkled, and my pen is running out of ink. My head is spinning. Actually, I think that I am developing a slight migraine.

I am in Tokyo (yes, Tokyo, Japan), sitting on a bench in one of their well-celebrated gardens, writing. I am always writing. I suppose it is my therapy.

I am writing about you. I am smiling just with thinking. Can you remember the day we first met? I can honestly say I was not that interested in you, nor were you in me. Honestly, I gave you and three other people my number (bet you didn't know that). You called first. I'm glad you did.

And so we started talking—I, in analogies. Isn't it funny how I've always talked in analogies? You were pretty forward and honest; I admired that. There are a lot of fake people in this world. You were real to me, and right off the bat, I loved you for that. You tolerated my analogies (understood a few of them, too) and encouraged me—challenged me—to speak my mind. I had been hiding behind them, and you, being the perceptive individual you are, saw right through me. I became vulnerable to you, and you to me, but we didn't take advantage of each other, as some people might.

Sometimes, when I'm walking down a street, whether in the city or my own town, I wonder how people see me. Our world is composed of stereotypes—each person carries his or her views like a shield. Isn't it funny how people are afraid of differences? But when we were together, I never wondered what people thought. It just didn't matter. You were a Colombian boy, clean-cut and good-looking, who loved football. I was a light-haired, light-skinned Catholic-school girl who loved art and writing. I hadn't the foggiest idea about football.

Life was sweet. But, of course, as there always is a silver lining, there can also be a thunderstorm. I began to notice some of my friends' lack of support. My best friends (even though some did not agree with interracial dating) were still supportive. But some strongly opposed it. I tried to explain my problem to you, but I just couldn't speak. Isn't it ironic how such a verbal person can become mute at such imperative times? I remained silent as it grew worse.

You are wondering what got worse? First, people began to make jokes. They were horrible, yet I blamed their cruelty on "ignorance." I use "ignorance" as an excuse when, in reality, ignorance is quite often a choice.

The incident that I remember most vividly (even to this day) happened in chemistry class. One lab period we were working with chemicals including iodine. Iodine taints your skin black or dark brown if you come in contact with it. My teacher warned us about it. She didn't want us to stain our uniforms.

A few minutes later, I heard a loud voice recommend that I dye my skin black so I could be like my boyfriend. I froze.

That is all I can think of now: those words. I hear them almost every day, sometimes over and over, like a bad dream, a broken record. Those were not words of ignorance; those were words of hate. And it makes me so sad, so sad.

But I am glad that we have not let them win. Isn't it funny how people can take something as simple and beautiful as love and turn it into a struggle? I can honestly say that I would gladly repeat all those nights I cried myself to sleep. A friendship like yours is worth more than any of that . . . much, much more.

And so, maybe we have won; I am not ashamed to come forward and say that I love you with all my heart, and that it would never matter to me whether you were white . . . black . . . or purple. Because love, my friend, sees no colors. Love sees no colors. ▣

After I Left

by Michelle Wedig

I never told you what happened after I left, did I? I knew I was never going to see you again. It really didn't matter, anyway. Tomorrow you would be on a bus for Connecticut and I would be here, alone. I didn't know what I was feeling. Was I supposed to be sad? Was I supposed to be happy? The only feeling I had was uncertainty.

It had been raining. I could still feel the moisture in the air, but the clouds were gone. The wet black asphalt reflected the street lamps and flower petals from the trees stuck to the brick sidewalk. I walked quickly down Springfield Street. I could hear the screams resonating from Center Street. A party was going on in one of the apartments. Police sirens echoed in the background. The city was still alive, but I didn't feel part of it anymore.

I came to the train station and took a left to the park. I could see the red neon arches of the station. A man in his mid-twenties was lying on the grass with a white husky, staring into the darkness of night. He asked me what time it was. I didn't have a watch, so I told him I didn't know.

Maybe he was feeling the way I was. I wanted to ask him what he felt. I wanted to ask him if we could talk. I wanted to tell him he had the most beautiful dog in the world. But I just continued toward the station, without another word.

I hurried along the sidewalk. A group of kids my age passed me. One of them asked me for a cigarette. I told him I was sorry, but I didn't have any. Then he asked me if I had any spare change. His friends giggled and some were embarrassed that he could even ask such a question. To his surprise I asked him to hold out his hands and I emptied my pockets of all the change that you had paid me back. I think it was about three dollars of nickels. I didn't need it. It was probably going to sit in a jar on my desk for five years until I had some dire need for nickels. The kid thanked me profusely. I had given him enough to buy his own cigarettes and a soda.

I made my way to the station. I glanced at the clock as I ran down the stairs to Track Three. I had two minutes to spare. I watched people until the train came. Nothing was interesting or unique about them. They were all suburbanites thrown into the city for different reasons and now they had to go home.

The train rolled in. The wheels came to an earsplitting halt that left me partially deaf. The conductor gave his usual spiel.

"This is the Clinton local, stopping at Southbridge, Middleboro, Canton. . . ."

I got on the train and found an empty seat. I noticed a girl across the aisle. She looked like me—it was really odd. I tried to listen to her conversation, but she was speaking some Slavic language I couldn't decipher. Maybe she was some long-lost relative from Eastern

Europe. I didn't think so; every one of my relatives had been killed in the Holocaust.

I forgot about the girl and put on my Walkman. "Hurt" by Nine Inch Nails was playing. I wondered if it were appropriate for the mood I was in. No, it didn't fit. I wasn't that upset. You were gone, and I had to move on or else I would be caught up in another depression. You weren't worth being that sad. The summer was coming, and it was almost a job requirement for me to be happy. You didn't affect me that much. I smiled at that thought. My mom always said that I was too easily influenced and I didn't have a mind of my own. I proved her wrong this time. It made me happy to prove my mom wrong.

"Clinton!" the conductor hollered.

I got off the train and walked to my car. I didn't cry when I left your apartment, knowing that I'd never see you again. I'll never cry for you. ⊡

The Question

Fiction by Ena Chang

T he trip to the restaurant began in silence. She sat in the back seat staring at the beads of water dancing on the windshield in the wind. Her father chuckled, and her mother changed the radio station. They talked about the work involved in redecorating the living room. Leslie didn't pay any attention to the conversation—she had other things on her mind.

Tonight was the night. She had to ask him. Leslie knew that he would be working tonight and had persuaded her parents to try this restaurant in hopes of seeing him. But seeing him wasn't the only reason she wanted to go there; she had to talk to him. She'd known Jesse for more than twelve years, since he lived down the street from her. But ever since freshman year, she had hardly talked to him especially since she had switched to an all-girls school and he had gone on to the public high school. Oh, she'd seen him occasionally on weekends when he was out in his driveway washing his car. They'd wave, but she had never taken the initiative to say anything more than "hi." Now Leslie wished she'd chatted with him those times; it would have made tonight's visit so much easier. "He won't say 'yes,'" she muttered to herself, inwardly cringing at the thought.

"Did you say something, Hon?" her mother's voice floated to the back.

"No, Mom. Just talking to myself," she answered.

Her father's voice boomed, "So, Leslie, I hear the prom's coming, huh? So who's the unlucky guy?"

"Dad!" she moaned and then hurriedly changed the subject. "I heard that this restaurant has the best baked stuffed shrimp."

"Well, I think I feel like steak tonight," her father declared, parking the car. "Here we are!"

Leslie began to feel anxious; she could feel her stomach knotting up as she rehearsed the words in her mind over and over again. *Wanna go . . . no . . . Would you like . . . no . . . can you?* Maybe she shouldn't ask just yet. Maybe after dinner would be better. That way, she wouldn't feel stupid during the meal in case he said no. Or like her best friend Nancy suggested, she could casually "forget" her purse and then ask for Jesse when she retrieved it.

Her father held open the door for her mother and Leslie and they walked in.

"How many people? Three? Oh, hi Leslie, I haven't seen you in a while." Jesse looked up from the counter, flashing a warm smile.

Her mother said, "Hello there, I didn't know you had a job here. Working hard, I see. And how are your mom and dad?"

"They're doing fine." He led the way to the back of the restaurant. "We're not that busy tonight. Here are your menus."

Leslie watched the back of his blond head weave back to the front desk. Suddenly, she announced, "Be right back. I have to go to the ladies' room." She slowly passed his desk and hesitated, but Jesse's back was turned. Quickly, she marched to the bathroom.

Nervously, Leslie washed her hands and then peered into the mirror. Pushing a strand of brown hair back, she took a deep breath. *I'll do it,* she decided, gritting her teeth, *even if it kills me.*

She left the room confidently and approached Jesse. "Hi, Jesse," she breathed. "How've you been?"

"Leslie, hey!" His clear blue eyes twinkled. "Pretty good, but I can't wait 'til senior year's over and summer's here. These last few months have been draggin', if you know what I mean. So tell me, what's happening in your life?"

"The usual . . . nothing. Jesse? Um . . . listen, can I ask you a huge favor?"

"Sure, ask away," he said, his blue-blue eyes beaming even more.

"Well, what are you doing May 18? I mean . . . what I want to say is, are you? Well . . . I want to know if you would care to go to my senior prom with me," she blurted, twisting her hands nervously behind her back.

"Are you kidding?" he grinned. "I'd love to go."

"You would? I mean, hey, that's great," Leslie exclaimed with a sigh of relief.

"Hey, if you ever feel like getting married, call me, okay?" he laughed, his tan face crinkling.

"Yeah, right," Leslie brightened, her light brown eyes lighting up as she made her way back to her table. *Yes!*

she thought to herself and her face started to jerk into a grin in spite of herself.

Later when her father put the tip on the table and they started to leave, he tried again. "Y'know, Leslie, are you sure you don't want to take me as your prom date?" he teased.

"Sorry, Dad. No need to," she returned, heading toward the exit. "I already have a date."

"You do?" he asked, astonished.

Leslie waved good-bye to Jesse; he winked back.

"Uh-huh," she sang. ▣

2 Ballads of Love

Photo by Sarah Roberto

The First

by Dana Rusk

I close my eyes and there we are
in a hotel parking lot
on the roof of your car
hoping it doesn't cave in
Dancing slowly
even to the fast songs
You kissed me softly
You said you loved me
You brought tears to my eyes
Sometimes you still do
And if I can't be the only one
To leave high heel marks
on your car
on your heart
At least I know
I was the first

Beauty in the Trivial Things

by Kenneth L. Flewelling

I stand there, my back to her,
her thin arms wrap around my waist.
And she rests her chin on my shoulder,
dark auburn hair flows down like thick syrup.
And I find I want to taste her again,
one sweet breath of fragrance and she holds me.
Whispers melt against my neck,
draining into my ear and it tickles
as it slowly trickles
down to where they lie silently.
Her warmth seeps into my body,
slowly killing the cold that covers me.
And I pray for this never to end,
beauty in the trivial things.

October Ache

by Beth Anne Nadeau

I feel it now,
that cold October ache
that comes only
with the change of seasons
and the absence of you.
I sense your presence
dripping from me slowly,
more and more as
each day passes
and the miles between us
make little effort
to shrink.

Without your company,
it is a chore to smile
and impossible to laugh.
Without your warmth,
it is not enough
to dress in layers
and crank the heat until
my parents yell at my foolishness
and turn it back down.

Since you have been gone,
art has lost its soul
and music has had no bass line.
My toast is dry now that
you are not here.
Nothing is the same
and I forget how it used to be.

I had a dream
that you came home.
We watched TV and argued
like always
and I smiled and laughed again.
Funny how you can do in dreams
what you've forgotten how to do
in real life.

I miss you, and I mean that.
I miss the glow that
surrounds you and always would
rub off, just a little,
on me. Without you
part of me is gone
and that cold October ache
fills me like a sickness.

A Turtle-Shaped Box

by Daniel Bailey

I had a dream the other day
That you'd driven me to madness—
Obviously I couldn't tell it was a dream—
I dreamt that, in frustration and despair,
I pulled the broken heart from my chest
Half of it I sautéed with mushrooms,
Garnished with asparagus
And partook of my own Last Supper.
The other half I UPSed to you,
Its former owner.
I admit
(you always know when I'm lying anyway),
A small piece I saved,
To appease the sniveling, sentimental moron
Inside me who still hopes you'll come back,
And I put that piece in a turtle-shaped box
On my chest-of-drawers.
This was symbolic—
Some people used to believe that
The Earth was held up by a great turtle—
You were my world . . . but not anymore.

I woke up with a strange feeling of pleasure
But I was just as miserable as when
I had brushed my teeth and gotten into bed the night
*   before.*
I wished my dream was real—
You can't live without a heart,
It's very similar to trying to
Live without you.
I wish I was an ostrich so
I could bury my head in the ground.

Photo by Brian Wayne

We Drive on the Endless Road

by Chelsea Lettieri

We drive on the endless road,
not a soul
in my vision,
only him and me.

The car,
blazing red like fire,
And small,
our seats near each other.

Music loud and lovely
Playing a song:
"You will never know,
the one who loves you so . . ."

He starts to sing along.
The words become a mystery.
The sound of his voice is all I can hear.
Sweet,
like the smell of a cake baking.

He puts his hand out,
and pats my head
gently,
as if trying not to break me.

But he does.

He breaks my heart
every time he looks at me,
because I know
we are only friends.
And that is all we will ever be.

We continue to drive on the endless road,
many people
in his vision:
me,
and the whole rest of the world.

Waiting

by Rachel Weiner

i sink into
the squeaky brown leather couch,
the black screen of the television glares at me
and the obnoxious floral wallpaper dances behind
*   my head.*
i relax
and you comfort me in your chicken noodle soup
*   warmth.*

i place my head on your patient chest
and your heartbeat slows as your body settles.
i reach up and untuck the curl from behind your ear,
smooth life into each strand of tired hair with
*   my fingertips.*
i sigh
and my tongue unchains my thoughts at last.

i mumble about my slowly fading friends,
my angered family,
misunderstandings,
disbeliefs,
the stereotypes about us
written in their untrusting eyes

these i am pelted with until i drown
in the bitter thoughts.

your lips against my head soothe me
they thirst for mine
and we touch . . .

"it's love that they doubt," i whisper,
(your love still lingers at the corners of my mouth)
"and I listen to their doubts,
believe the experienced and long-trusted."

so perhaps you and i are wrong?
we are not one, but two
we do not love, we lust
it will not last, i'll lose—
"i know," your eyes sing at me,
"that i love you."
i am silent
and i stare into your scarred hand
that rests on my wrist ever so gently—
it almost reminds me of your kisses.
i know i love you, too.

so while their shouts lurk in the corners,
i escape into our often dreamed-of future
or onto that static phone-line connection
or that caramelized leather sofa
waiting in your basement.

Six O'Clock Now

by Joyce Sun

six o'clock now
we should be together
in some soft, quiet place
of maples unleafing onto the
blue blue sky.

> *six o'clock now*
> *you should be parting the*
> *hair off my face*
> *with those eggshell thin fingertips,*
> *occasionally laying a kiss along the*
> *fixed joint of my skull.*

six o'clock now
I should be watching you
in the pale gray light
a line of white in a landscape
of black shadow.

> *six o'clock now*
> *you should be holding my hand*
> *in a grove of sycamores unleafing*
> *and we should be—*
> *we should be*
> *listening to the breath of golden*
> *autumn fading into*
> *the darkening wood.*

Kiss

by Kendra Lider-Johnson

We laughed in the dark
but inside I was silent.
There was not enough light for me to see you
and I saw monsters.
Too many pregnant moments between us
were miscarried. There was no blood.
There was nothing.
Our arms empty of each other.
I atrophy.
Do you see me wither? I die,
and your hands are too soft,
I wasn't ready.
You play with my heart when you kiss me.
Then you leave the room. Game over.
Better luck next time.
I don't cry. I refuse to care.
The door is closed and
my eyes are closed.
I am empty. I try to smile, but can't.
The monsters are under my eyelids.

Sitting on Your Uncle's Porch

by Laura Dickinson

sitting on your uncle's front porch
we ate bag-ripened peaches
that tasted of georgia soil
not that we had firsthand experience
but in our own
california twilights
we found a sense of belonging
to ourselves
as well as to each other
my pink-and-white toes
interlaced
with your scarred brown
creating an appalachian landscape
of calluses and knuckles
do toes have knuckles?
no one knew the answer
but
it was better not to know
to let our minds drift
over such things
as toe-knuckles and sand dollars

you once
brought me twenty sand dollars
all teeny-tiny perfect
strung on a fishing wire
the most
beautiful necklace I'd ever got
didn't I love the way
you'd lean back, gangly-like
all over the steps
of your uncle's porch
limbs
carefully sprawled into a pose
that smacked of machismo
machismo at fifteen
was hard to come by then
not something
bought at a corner store
or found in an abandoned gutter
no sir
something earned
earned in a first kiss
I gave you on the porch steps
when you gave me
the last slice of peach
how chivalrous of you
I thought
so I rewarded you
with a small kiss—pretty big thing
sixteen-year-old kissing a
boy of only fifteen
but it was summer

only the fireflies
could whisper any stories
so I kissed you
and smiled
as you straightened up
blushed
and carefully arranged yourself again
composure supposedly unruffled
but
now you were metamorphosed
into a man
boy no longer
peach juice trickled down my wrist
I licked it off
aware
of eyes following my tongue
how hot
a june evening can become.

Photo by Summer A. Miller

Rebecca

by Alexandra Berger

today
i loved you,
simply out of selfishness.
i was sick of myself
and everyone else
who i had been with for too long,
so long i could not remember.
and so i loved you,
because you were different from
all the others i had known.
because of your boldness;
your skin like the snow,
your mind like the ocean.
it was as though i was
stepping on swords,
as i tried to tame
your wild instincts.
silently
i screamed your name
but you were blinded by
your own exotic ways,
more exciting than my own.
and tomorrow,

where will we be tomorrow?
in the same starting square,
like plastic game pieces landing
where the board says, "go back"
like those stupid games that
keep kids entertained for hours.
for hours i have been chasing you,
your skin like the snow
your mind like the ocean,
and your smile.
not realizing
how misleading your eyes can be,
you smile.
and as i try to tame
your wild instincts,
i realize that i had loved you
simply out of selfishness.

Challenging Tales

Photo by Sandy Medeiros

Knowing When

by Lindsay R. Pattison

Tank tops, boxer shorts, newly designed hairdos and faces painted with all the wrong shades of makeup: another Saturday-night slumber party with best friends. Julie, Molly and I had been friends since Julie's mom forgot to pack her a snack the first day of fourth grade. Friends already, Molly and I agreed to share our half-eaten granola bars and chocolate milk with the new girl. None of us would ever have guessed that this act of kindness would lead to many potato chip–filled, secret-sharing nights.

Tonight, however, was different. We were edgy and nervous, quick to snap at each other. The carefree makeup escapades were over as we each tried to look our best and ravaged Molly's bathroom for the perfect shade of eye shadow. I stepped back once to notice the chaos that engulfed us, but quickly snapped back as Julie snatched the mascara from my hand. Molly, realizing Julie now possessed the key to long, luscious lashes, chased after her. I chuckled as I watched my two best friends run out the door.

Our playfulness had returned, and I joined in the wrestling match on the bed, the prize no longer mascara but the pure enjoyment of friendship. We were interrupted by the doorbell, and shrieked with anticipation. *They're here!* I thought. Rolling off the bed, we pushed and shoved for a small corner of the mirror to check our hair and makeup. With the second ring we cavorted down to the front door and anxiously waited for Molly to open it. She hesitated and looked at us uneasily. After all, we weren't just opening her front door, but beginning a whole new era. There would be dating, holding hands, kissing and heartbreak. The third ring reminded us that we couldn't back out now. Molly opened the door to three sweaty-palmed boys, obviously as nervous as we, and she invited them in.

Gathering in the living room, the three of us strategically placed ourselves around the table so that we were each next to the boy of our dreams. After sitting in silence for a minute, Molly offered drinks and all three boys accepted, probably out of hope that it would spark conversation. Julie, Molly and I glided toward the kitchen attempting to look as graceful as possible, but falling over each other as we got there, babbling in hushed whispers about "our boys." Regaining our composure we stepped back into the spotlight and rejoined them at the table.

"Got any cards?"

"Um, yeah, just a minute," Molly said as she leaned over and reached in a desk drawer. "Here you are," she said, flashing a smile as she handed them over.

"Poker, anyone?" one of the boys suggested. The three of us shot glances at each other knowing full well that none of us knew much about poker.

"Sure," Julie said, flashing a smile in her crush's

direction. I looked at the boy sitting next to me and smiled at him, almost out of obligation. Picking up my cards, I looked at them with a blank stare, not sure how they could work together to mean anything.

"Hey," the boy next to me said. "Look what I've got." Pulling a joint out of his pocket, he rolled it between his fingers as though admiring a precious gem. "I stole it from my brother's room, but he won't notice. He has tons. Wanna try it?" He thrust it toward me. All I could do was stare at it. I tried to say something, but when I opened my mouth, all that came out was air.

"Pass it this way," one of the other boys said. Lighting it, he took a puff and passed it to Julie. Nervously, she took it and inhaled. Not knowing what to expect, she inhaled too much and ended up coughing.

"Here, let me try," Molly said, grabbing the joint from Julie.

"All right, but let's play," one of the boys said, retrieving his cards from the table. Everyone else followed his lead and picked up their cards. Molly put the joint to her lips, inhaled and coughed just as Julie had. The boy between us laughed as he picked up the joint after Molly dropped it and took a puff himself. Next it was my turn. A hundred excuses and reasons ran through my mind. Focused on my cards, the red and black became a blur. I laid my cards facedown on the table.

"I fold." Getting up, I grabbed my coat. It was their turn to watch me walk out the door. ▣

Promises, Promises, Promises

by Jessica Gonzalez

The tears stream down my face, running into my mouth. I don't even notice the taste, but my heart feels heavy, weighted with guilt and shame. I can barely think straight, and I curl up in a ball, letting the sobs overcome me. After an eternity, I hear a knock at the door. It's my mom. She asks if I'm all right; I meekly say I am. Mom sees right through my words and attempts to comfort me, saying it wasn't my fault—Mrs. W was confused toward the end and wasn't angry with me. The words don't help. My guilt still surrounds me like a dark cloud, and I can't shut out the question running through my mind: *Why didn't I just keep my promise?*

* * *

The smell of freshly baked ginger-cinnamon cookies permeates the hallway. I run to the stove, eager to grab one. Mrs. Wojtowicz, a robust, smiling German woman, greets me with a thick accent, scolding me not to eat them; they are for my dad. Mrs. W is one of my dad's patients and feels immense gratitude to him for saving her life. Kindhearted woman that she is, she "adopted" me as a grandchild, having none of her own. She feels the only way to express her thanks is by letting me and my family into her heart. Being ten years old with no relatives nearby, I'm ecstatic. She bakes for the remainder of the day, and I'm perfectly happy to nap in the company of my surrogate grandma and her large, fluffy cats.

* * *

The years passed and Mrs. W never forgot a birthday or missed a dance recital. She was a constant, reassuring presence in my life. Whether we were baking, traveling or just talking, I always enjoyed my time with her. But as I grew older, certain things began to seem more important. It was time for boys instead of baking, friends instead of museums, and parties instead of long talks with a sweet woman who had no family.

Even though I had become more distant, she was still there for me with a warm hug and a plate of cookies. One thing Mrs. W and I had always wanted to do was have a fancy meal at the French Café. One cold November day, I decided I wasn't too wrapped up with my life and so we went. "Finally," she exclaimed, "I have taken my doll-baby to the French Café for fancy-fancy meal."

I just smiled patronizingly while she stared peacefully into space. My fifteen-year-old frame fidgeted restlessly. I should have been overjoyed that we were finally carrying out our fancy-party fantasy, but instead I was thinking about what I would be doing later that night. We ordered food we couldn't pronounce and laughed about old times before I was a teenage ball of hormones.

Before I knew it, it was time to leave. I looked up at my Mrs. W and saw tears forming in her kind blue eyes. I threw my arms around her, trying to coax out the truth. She finally confessed that she was upset that we didn't see each other as often since she moved an hour away. An idea came to me.

"Why don't I drive down to spend the weekend when I turn sixteen?" I suggested excitedly. The look on her face was my answer, and I promised her it was a date.

I remember that feeling of freedom the first few weeks after turning sixteen—the open road, no more parents carting me around . . . total independence. I let that feeling overtake me and let the promise I had made to her slip from my memory. Never a pushy person, she didn't remind me, hoping I would come when I was ready.

As it turns out, I never did visit Mrs. W. I never even said good-bye to one of my favorite people, which is why I have been balled up, sobbing, since my mom told me the news a few hours ago.

My mom explained that Mrs. W had been sick for a long time and seemed to be holding on until my visit. She had wanted to give me her jewelry and treasures before she died, not having a daughter or granddaughter of her own. I didn't know this. Mrs. W was aware of her impending death, but being a strong person, she never told me about her illness for fear it would upset me. When I didn't visit her month after month, her will to live started to fade, thinking she had done something to make me not want to see her. She died silently, from a broken heart, I feel.

As I lay sobbing, it dawned on me how incredibly important promises are. I realized that even though I could not bring her back, I could keep one promise. She had always wanted to donate money to the Humane Society where she found her beloved cats. Mrs. W could never spare any money. When she died, I decided to give the money she left me to the Humane Society to build a new cat room in her honor.

So, I am keeping the promise to take care of not only her cat but many others, and I know she would be happy about this. I know now that breaking a promise can lead to breaking a heart . . . and that's just too heavy a price to pay. ▣

Photo by Liz Cashman

My Father's Chevy

by Jamie Graham

He'd been drinking again. I could smell it on his breath the second he walked in the door. His thin hair was tangled, and his flannel shirt reeked of smoke. He stood for a few seconds, looking down at me sitting at the kitchen table. I knew what he was going to say even before the slurred syllables escaped his chapped lips.

"Why don't you come for a ride with me, Jame?"

It wasn't really a request, but a drunken demand. I pretended not to hear him. For me, hell could be described in three words: my father's Chevy. It was a rusted green prison-on-wheels where my father held me captive on summer nights in his attempt to spend quality time with his twelve-year-old daughter. He would drive aimlessly down country roads, holding the steering wheel in one hand and a sweating beer in the other, while I stared silently out of the cracked window at the sad night sky. I never spoke. Sometimes, if he was drunk enough, he would preach about politics or how the government was screwing him out of his hard-earned money. Other times, we'd just ride in awkward silence. I had come to loathe this ritual of father-daughter bonding and the man who forced it upon me.

He slammed his callused hand down on the table to get my attention.

"I said, why don't you come for a ride with me, Jamie Lynn?"

I knew better than to keep the man waiting. I rose stiffly from my chair and followed him out the front door into the summer night. The warm breeze teased my hair and whispered taunts into my ear. I felt like a prisoner being escorted by a merciless guard to a slow, agonizing death. Only this electric chair was twelve feet long and read "CHEV O ET" on the rusted tailgate. I climbed into the seat and strapped myself in.

Not a single word was said as we pulled out of the driveway. He quietly sipped his beloved beer while I stared into the darkness.

I did not know the lonely man sitting across from me, nor did I want to know him. He was a stranger. The only memory I had of my father was him conversing with the bottle. Any others had long ago been suffocated to a forgotten death by the hurt and the hate.

We rode on in silence.

He seemed so tense. Since my mom left us for another man last summer, my father has been lost in depression. He usually just nursed his suffering with a couple of Budweisers. Tonight, however, there was something different in how he sped around the curves of the gravel road. He seemed almost weary, as though every turn of the wheel caused him great pain and sadness.

I shifted uncomfortably in my seat. We were going much too fast. In all my late-night expeditions with him, I had never seen him like this. His sunburned face hung slack, while his tired eyes gazed into the unpromising distance. He mechanically brought his beer to his lips. I wondered if he realized that it had long ago been emptied.

Thundering silence.

We had been barreling down the dark road for twenty excruciating minutes when at last he cleared his throat.

"You know," he said, his eyes fixed straight ahead, "I never meant for any of this, Jame. You know that, right? Me and you, we used to be buddies. Remember?"

Once again, I shifted uncomfortably. We were going much too fast. I did not want to be there. In that truck. With him.

When my father realized I wasn't going to answer, he spoke again.

"Dammit, tell me you remember, Jame," he pleaded. "Please!"

I was beginning to get scared. Even at his most frightening, I had never seen him like this. My heart was racing like this truck through the darkness. I did not know what to do.

My mind quickly searched for something, anything, to say to this man who was my father.

What about all of those long nights that I spent crying as a child because Daddy never came home? What about the many times I'd wanted to tell him I loved him, but didn't know how? Once again, I couldn't find the words to save us.

We were going about ninety miles an hour now. His fingers gripped the steering wheel so hard that his knuckles were beginning to turn white. The engine thundered like a charging bull, demanding that I say something, but my lips stayed frozen.

This time my father turned to face me before speaking. There was a wild pain in his glossy, drunk eyes. "Jamie," his voice cracked, "me and you . . ."

I had never in my life seen my father cry, but now the tears came like an overdue baptism. His shoulders shook as he slowed the racing truck to a stop in the middle of the road and hunched over the cracked wheel, his head in his hands. Years of pain and drunken desperation poured out of him in violent sobs.

I touched his shoulder gingerly. He looked up at me, his eyes dripping with shame and embarrassment.

"Daddy," I whispered softly, "I remember." ▣

The Crying Room

by Catherine Zimmerman

November seventeenth changed everything for my friend, and for me.

I was working that day, enduring a typical Friday night of Christmas shoppers and crabby customers. I couldn't wait to leave. My boyfriend had just gotten a job at the same mall, and we were planning to meet for dinner at nine o'clock. It was snowing, and I watched the delicate flakes fall and cling to the mall's glass double-doors. It was the first snow of the season, and I would have to adjust to driving home in winter weather.

I shuffled a stack of sale flyers at my register. It was really coming down now. The snowy roads would make driving difficult.

"Hello," I chimed to an elderly lady with a plaid handkerchief tied around her head and a cane in hand. She smiled, making her wrinkled face smooth in what seemed a rare moment of happiness. I felt sorry for older people; it must be lonely growing old, considering the things you've done in life, the things you've missed. How short life is when you really stop to think about it. I wish people never grew old. I had lost my great-grandma, and though I didn't understand it at seven, I understood now and loathed the inevitable.

Suddenly, the ringing of the phone interrupted my thoughts.

"Hello, JCPenney. This is Cathy speaking."

Silence.

"Hello?"

Uncontrollable sobbing blared from the other end.

"Who is this?" I asked, an awful feeling coming over me.

"This is Corrina," an unstable voice stammered.

"Okay," I began, trying to be calm. "Where are you, Honey?"

"I'm at the hospital," she stuttered, tension building in her voice. I knew she wouldn't be able to hold it together much longer.

"Where in the hospital?" I asked.

"In the emergency room." A cough and more crying followed the empty words. "My dad just died. . . ."

I covered my mouth with one hand as I stood there hanging onto the counter. I felt nauseous, hollow. As I regained my composure, I began to speak.

"Okay, I'll be right there—right there, okay?"

"Okay," she sobbed.

I was shaking. I felt as if I should be doing five things at once. Thoughts ran rampant through my head as I prepared to leave work.

Okay, first, let Jan know you're leaving, then just drive.

How could this have happened? He was fine two days ago.

I stormed out the front doors and started for my car.

The cold wind hit my face as I turned the key to open my car door. I slammed the door and turned the key. It was so cold that my car sputtered.

Come on, start.

I turned the key again. The engine finally hummed as my hands gripped the icy steering wheel.

Don't drive stupidly, Cathy. You're not going to be any help if you don't get there in one piece.

I pulled out of my parking space and drove toward the nearest exit.

Take a right.

I felt as if I should be driving an emergency vehicle.

Turn right again.

I was on the highway now. It wouldn't be much longer before I reached the hospital.

There it is.

I turned into the emergency entrance.

Was she there alone? She had been too upset to dwell on details, and I had been too shocked to ask. All I could think of was getting to her as quickly as possible. She had called me, of all people. We had grown up together; she was the sister I'd never had. We had done everything together.

I moved here when I was seven, a scared little girl with no friends. When I entered the first-grade classroom two weeks after the school year started, every kid looked at me like I had transferred from another planet. I remember the teacher introducing me: "Class, this is Cathy Zimmerman. She just moved here and will be going to school with us."

I smiled shyly and looked around the room. No one

smiled back. They all looked down and began coloring again—no expression, no hello. I hung up my coat and took my seat.

I spent the next few years going to school and spending summers watching cartoons and "swimming" in my Little Mermaid wading pool. There were no girls my age in the neighborhood, and Mom said the boys played too rough after I came home crying with a black eye from a baseball game. On occasion, I'd ride my "cool" purple ten-speed bicycle around the neighborhood. I could make it around the block with no hands—corners and all—a great accomplishment for a ten-year-old.

One day I had just made it to the first stop sign of my loop when I saw another little girl riding behind me. I waited for her to catch up. Strange noises were coming from her bicycle; I looked down to see a playing card flapping in the spokes of her tire.

"Whatchya got there?" I asked curiously, attempting conversation. "That thing in your tire. What's it for?"

"It's a card I found in the junk drawer at my house. You should see it! I bet you can find just about anything in there."

"I'd like that," I said, "but I'll have to ask my mom first."

I sped home as fast as my skinny chicken legs could take me. Mom said yes, and that was the beginning of my friendship with Corrina. From that day when I was ten and she was eight, we were inseparable. After a few years, I was thought of as another member of her family. I went on their vacations, ate most of my meals there and even slept there at least once a week. Her parents, Ellen and Roger, became my second mom and dad. Now this news had come out of nowhere and landed on our laps, an unreal night of cold, snow and death.

The parking lot was slippery; the ice itself could have hospitalized you. I skated to the glass door. I had only been here once, two years before, when Dad had a pain in his arm. The doctors diagnosed a joint disease. His hands ached constantly. You could see it in his eyes as he reached to drink another mouthful of coffee. Just gripping the mug caused his eyes to water. He was doing better now, and the medication helped him do his day-to-day activities. I wanted to go home and hug him, tell him how much I love him. I had taken for granted the importance of a father—until now.

Though I still had my dad, I felt like I had lost another. Roger, a man I also called Dad, would no longer be there for Saturday fishing trips, to tease me about my love life, or to take Corrina and me for ice cream.

I cautiously pushed open the doors. I could hear a baby crying. A man sat with his hand wrapped in a white cloth, trying to keep a small child from getting in the way of the swinging door I had entered. My presence was met with blank stares: people trying to see what was wrong with me, why I was there.

"Excuse me," I said to a nurse, "could you tell me if the Spengler family is here?"

Her lip-glossed smile turned into the most serious expression I had ever seen. "Oh, certainly, if you could just come with me." I saw sympathy in her face. I followed her through the white halls of the hospital. A man wheezed in one of the side rooms. The repetitive hacking made me cringe. It was the sound of death.

The nurse finally reached the door leading out of the never-ending maze of white walls. White was the color of spiritualism; these walls should have been painted black. This was the "Crying Room," a place for those who had just lost a loved one. This room ensured they would be alone while they grieved and made the necessary phone calls. This was where they sent you to cry, to gather your thoughts. I wondered how many people had come here before us to compose themselves after terrible news.

I cautiously entered. They sat, gathered around a table with a phone book and telephone in the middle of their circle. Corrina peeked out from behind the door. It was cramped in there. All the people made it hard to breathe. No words were exchanged between us. She began to cry again, and I hugged her tightly as she clung to my collar. There was nothing I could say. I had never felt so help-less. I stood there and held her, shedding tears on the crying-room floor. ▣

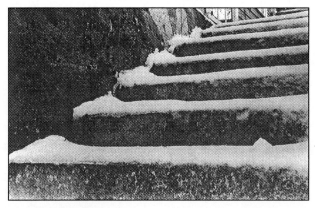

Photo by Brian Wayne

Blood Is Thicker Than Water

by Faheem Robinson

I never thought that my sister would really run away. But I guess I thought wrong. It all started that fall. I came home from school and noticed she wasn't there. I didn't think anything of it at first, but soon it would be dark.

Hours passed and my dad started to get worried. He got on the phone and called just about everyone he knew. Then, just as we were going out to look for her, my aunt called telling us that my sister was going to move in with her because she needed a female role model in her life. (My mother had left the scene when I was born.) But all I heard that night was: "Hell no, she can't have my daughter." Next thing I knew my dad was telling me to get dressed—we were going to my aunt's house.

When we arrived, I had never seen my dad so angry. He looked like he was going to blow. I didn't know what was going on; all I was thinking about was going to bed. When my dad got to the front porch, my aunt came to the door and said that my sister didn't want to see him because she thought he was going to yell at her.

Meanwhile, I sat in the car watching my dad and my aunt argue. All of a sudden, my dad walked to the end of the driveway, picked up a brick and smashed my aunt's front car window.

My aunt didn't get mad, she just called the cops. While they were still arguing, the cops came and arrested my dad on the spot. They treated him like he was a kid. I couldn't do anything; all I did was cry like a hungry baby. They threw him to the ground like an animal, tightened the handcuffs on his wrists and then threw him to the ground again. My dad tried fighting back, but three to one were not even odds. The last words I remember my dad saying were: "Go in the house, Faheem." Then he turned to the cops and said: "My son doesn't need to be seeing this." Then the officer flung my dad into the back of the squad car.

The next morning I was in a sorry state of mind. Social workers and cops were asking me all sorts of questions. I didn't answer; they all looked evil to me with their fake smiles and want-to-help attitudes. I thought to myself, *If you want to help me, let my father out of jail.*

Since then, my life has changed drastically. The state took us away from my father because they said we were living in a bad environment, and that they had found drugs in our house, which kept my father away longer. Then they put us in a foster home, then another, then another and another. Finally, we ended up with another aunt who lived nearby.

Life was cool with my aunt, but I had to adjust to the way people lived in her town. Everything was fine until her husband started complaining about how he didn't want to raise more children. Some family . . . huh? My aunt got sick of hearing him complain about raising more children so she put us back in a foster home.

Luckily for me and my sister, a neighbor two houses down from my aunt's stepped in. My sister was already friends with their daughter. Her parents called the state and said that they would like to take custody of us. I love them for that.

But it seems weird that a total stranger can take us in and show us love that my own family couldn't. The strange part about it is that we live only two houses from my aunt, but she doesn't visit or call us.

As I write this, I'm much older and wiser. I miss my dad with all my heart and wish he were out so he could see me graduate. But that wish will never come true. I will always wonder if my sister had not run away, would I still be with my dad. Sometimes I blame her for losing him and sometimes I blame my aunt. But what I do know is that my family will never be the same. I went through a lot of heartache and suffering, but suffering builds character. Whoever said that "blood is thicker than water" lied. ◙

Taking Control

by Heather Quinn

I t's so hard to go through life when you look in the mirror every day and hate what you see. Violently and passionately hate. For me, this hatred turned into starvation, or self-destruction. I weighed one hundred and eight pounds at five feet, two-and-a-half inches when I decided I was desperately fat. That was all I saw when I looked in the mirror. I saw childhood scars. When I was growing up, my father had a drinking problem and deserted us. I guess this was my way of showing all the unsettled pain I was feeling.

In almost all cases of anorexia, there is an underlying reason to propel someone to starve, to commit slow suicide. Essentially, anorexia is suicide, painful in the same way. Anorexia is so powerful; for me, it was all I had. I woke up and was disgusted with the way I saw myself. I thought everything made me look fat, so I began skipping breakfast, then lunch. Soon, I ate one small meal a day and became very weak. I did vigorous exercising every day but still it wasn't enough. I wasn't getting enough attention; nobody was noticing. My cry for attention was being ignored, and I still thought of myself as disgusting.

When I reached a hundred pounds, I decided to start

using laxatives. My stomach was constantly cramped, but my head told me it was absolutely necessary. I had to be thin, because once I was thin, everything would be okay. I wouldn't ever feel unloved or hurt. I would be beautiful and happy.

Happy was something I hadn't been in a long time. Ever since I started my diet, I had been sad. I was always feeling sick or at least sick of myself. I barely ever saw friends, since I exercised all the time instead. I thought my friends were jealous when they commented on my weight so I just disassociated myself from them. I was alone a lot so there was no one to tell me *not* to stick my finger down my throat whenever I ate. Burning my throat almost every day didn't matter; this stuff, food, was going to make me fat, so it had to be eliminated, in any way possible.

I was so far gone that I couldn't even see myself anymore. If people told me I looked sick, I took it as a compliment. It was so hard because, even when I stopped hurting myself, the feelings were still there. They always will be; they haunt me almost every day, each time I look in the mirror or hear someone say they are on a diet.

But even now, it's hard for me to say I had a problem. In my head, I was always too fat to be suffering from anorexia, but that in itself defines the disease. My best friend sat me down one day and told me she wasn't going to let me kill myself; my mother found my laxatives; and my world crashed down around me. I had no control when I thought I had it all. I was so blinded by my perceptions, I couldn't function. It's the same with any addiction: It takes over and makes your whole life revolve around it. The lies were backfiring and I fainted so often, it was unreal, but nobody wanted to say I had a problem, especially me. Finally, my friend got through to me; I stopped the diet pills and laxatives. I was extremely lucky to be able to do it alone, without hospitalization.

I am nowhere near cured. I know that, but I've stopped. I now have control. I face a battle every day at each meal. I still diet, but I am so thankful to be alive. I almost killed myself. At ninety pounds, I almost died because of a diet, one taken to an extreme because of my own life, my emotional state, my fears and my thirst for control. They almost got the best of me. But luckily, I fought back, and I think, right now, I'm winning. ◙

Photo by Lena Koroleva

The Great Teacher

by Adrienne A. Perry

aying it's wonderful to see me again, you plop down in your chair as I catch a quick breath of air.

"Your hair . . . ," I say, for you look nothing like my memories of you two years ago, before the cancer came.

"I told you that chemotherapy gave me a built-in crew cut," you joke in a thick German accent, for if there is one trait that the Grim Reaper didn't claim, it is your sense of humor.

Reaching out my hand, I feel the scarce fuzz of what used to be a full head of thick hair. You used to be so proud of it, never allowing a strand to fall out of place. I had secretly admired it for years, but never told you because I thought your ego was too big already. I'm sorry now for thinking that. I'm sorry for every time I thought you were annoying. I'm sorry for being selfish and not writing when I found out you had cancer, just because I didn't know what to write to a dying boy of sixteen. I wish now that I had scrawled anything, anything at all, like how happy I was when Sean came back from California, or about the cute little puppies our dog had, and how excited I was when Mom let us keep one I named Keenen.

I want you to know that every time I look outside the music-room window and see the field and trees swaying in the wind against a blue sky background, I think of you and wish you were here to see it. You taught me to appreciate sunny days, green grass and people playing soccer.

You taught me what death was, the finality of it, and how important it is to show people that I care about them. In many aspects, you were the greatest teacher I've ever had, without even knowing it.

Do you remember the time we got the buzz from the champagne and strawberries at our family reunion? We thought that we were smart when we put twelve glasses of it together, even though we must have spilled half of it tripping down the hill. Didn't we have fun? Do you remember paddle-boating to the middle of Bear Pond and telling me you were in love with Jenny, even though she hadn't even said two words to you? How about when I got mad at you for teaching Devon how to swear in German? I wish I hadn't yelled at you now, and I wish most of all that you didn't have to leave so soon. Would you like some more Coke? You told me once that American Coke was better than German Coke. If you would just stay, I'd give you all of the Coke you want. No, I understand, you have to go. Maybe I'll see you again someday. Until then, I'll be thinking of you. 回

Like Father, Not Like Son

by J. A. Gaeta

t first I could not fathom the fact that my father was in jail, all because he was drinking. My family thought he had given it up. It had been a factor in my parents' divorce. And now, after his ninety-day sentence, he was being released.

I had thought about this moment, this confrontation, and had dreaded it. So, the first weekend of his release, I called him. I asked how he thought he could get away with this. How could he risk the lives of innocent people as well as his own? I told him he was a horrible father, that he was an alcoholic and many other painful things. He did not try to minimize his mistakes. All he did was apologize and cry. He begged for my forgiveness and said, "Sorry, I love you," but I hung up. I was angry and pitied him, but I could not forgive him.

His drinking had never been a mystery. I remember him driving after a few drinks. Then four years ago, he was pulled over and charged with DWI (driving while intoxicated). He paid a hefty fine and his license was suspended for ninety days. One week after he was issued a new one he was pulled over again, his second DWI in six months. The courts were not lenient. He was given an even heftier fine, his driving privileges were revoked for three years and he was sentenced to ninety days in jail.

The next three months were tough. I couldn't believe this was my father. It was hard for a fourteen-year-old boy to think of his father in jail. It was harder to forgive him. Then I thought that only bad people did bad things and now my father was one of those bad people. I had nightmares about him and started to remember the things I wished he had done differently.

Now, three years later, my dad is back on the road with a new license and a new outlook on life. He has cleaned himself up (with the help of AA meetings and self-help) and is a recovering alcoholic. His job is going well, as is his relationship with the rest of the family. He has met a wonderful woman and they're engaged. Now he rarely touches a drink. Once in a while he will have half a beer, but then remembers the pain and hurt he caused. Now he does not want to jeopardize his relationship with anyone.

I, too, have a different outlook. I am almost eighteen, not that fourteen-year-old having nightmares. I have matured. I have a girlfriend and a fabulous relationships with my mother and stepfather. Through many experiences, learning about alcohol abuse and addiction, I have come to realize that my father is not alone and his problem is not all his fault.

All of these events, including an infinite number of "sorrys" and "please forgive mes," have caused me to begin to change my attitude toward my father. I have started thinking about what I can do to have a better relationship with him. I can also remember all the things he did for me and the good times we had. Slowly, I've started to see my father for who he is—a loving person who wants desperately to do the right thing. We've talked about all of this. I've accepted his apology, and he is grateful.

It is still hard being with him sometimes, but our relationship is improving. We get together a few days each month to talk and have a good time. In a strange way it's better now. We are more like good friends than father and son. I feel now that I can talk to him and he can give me advice. He never shouts at me for doing anything wrong, because of his past mistakes. He knows that and it may bother him, but he realizes his mistakes and where I'm coming from. We enjoy this new relationship and don't take anything for granted. I do care for my father, but I have seen the life he chose, and I do not want to end up like him. I never wish to follow in his footsteps. ◙

Entering Adult Territory

by Lindsey E. Cronin

Paramedics. Open door three, please," the speaker on the wall squawks. As I press the button to open the door I ask, "Where are you headed?"

"334."

Apartment 334. In a heartbeat, I know. Norman. My Norman. I grab my keys and fly through the building like a crazed woman, my mind racing.

When I got my job at the front desk of the retirement community, I was ecstatic. The lazy teenager in me took over. No more being on my feet eight hours straight serving meals or tolerating the old ladies who could never be pleased. No more killing my back lifting trays piled high with "spillables" or having to clean refrigerators or vacuum at the end of my shift. I could kick back behind the desk, answer a couple of phone calls and still get paid a dollar more an hour!

I met Norman during my dining-room days. Every mealtime, thirty minutes early, there he was at table five by the window. I'd walk past and he'd holler, "Why don't you pull up a chair and stay a while?" Not long after he sat down, his friend Paul would wander in and sit across from him. They were exact opposites, Norm and Paul.

Paul was a sweet, angelic old man the residents called "St. Paul" for putting up with "that old grump, Norman."

Norm played the "rotten troublemaker" part to a T. But he was lonely and in constant need of love, though you'd never hear him say it. I gave him the love he needed and the attention nobody else would. When he had to wait three hours at the doctor's office for a taxi all alone after hours, I cried for his loneliness. When he forgot the notebook that was his "life" at an appointment, I drove to get it for him. He would give me advice about my boyfriend, saying "dump that jerk" and watch over me, saying, "You don't look good today."

"Well, thank you, Norman," I'd say. "Not all of us can be as pretty as you."

"Oh, shut up. Here, take my keys and go take a nap on my couch while Paul and I eat our breakfast. We can take care of ourselves for a while."

"Norman! I have to work. Hush and eat your eggs."

We took care of each other. Now I'm racing up the stairs because I need to take care of him.

The police are outside his door, where his much-loved scooter sits. The paramedics are just standing there. He must be okay, or they would be rushing around. I ask what happened.

"Heart attack. Passed out on the bathroom floor. You have his medical card so we know what he was taking?" I hand it to him.

"Will he be all right?" I ask.

They look at me.

"He passed away sometime yesterday evening, we think around seven o'clock."

"Oh, okay," I hear myself say. I turn around, and already tears are streaming down my cheeks. The trip up to his apartment that had felt so long seems mere seconds as I make my way back. Too soon I am at my desk.

When the person from the morgue arrives, the police officer asks me to "come back up and give us a hand." I again make the journey to apartment 334. I haul his scooter into the apartment and help put Norman in the body bag and onto the gurney. I look at Norman.

I'm sorry I couldn't take care of you this time, Norman. I'm sorry you needed me and I wasn't there. Thank you for living as long as you did. I love you, and I'll never forget you, I tell him silently. The police officer distracts me from my thoughts and asks, "How old are you?"

"Seventeen."

"God, a seventeen-year-old seeing this stuff. What's the world coming to?"

Now I try not to fall in love with these residents because each time I lose one, I lose a part of myself. When I gave up the responsibilities of the dining room, I gave up my childhood as well. Now I have to see adult things, do adult things and handle things like an adult.

In the end, the desk job is harder. ◙

Hurtful Words

by Margot Leifer

Maybe it was the way she never stopped talking about her "perfect" boyfriend, or the far-fetched stories she seemed to fabricate. Whatever it was, we hurt her. We stabbed her in the back and watched as she doubled over. I would love to say that I wasn't responsible, but even though I only followed and laughed, I was an accomplice and just as guilty as the others with their hurtful words and cruel jokes.

Her boyfriend was away at college and because of his absence, she had been catapulted back into our lives. Once she had been so daringly exuberant, so full of energy, but going out with him for two years had affected her. She began to stay in the shadows, was reluctant to have fun and laughed less. She was an outsider—we had lost her for those two metamorphic years. We had our "in" jokes that she wasn't a part of.

Then she changed again and invited herself everywhere. When she did not get all the attention she now longed for, she would make up outrageous stories of Arabian women yelling "Black power" in the middle of Macy's or of Jujitsu fighters bringing back their opponents' ears for their girlfriends. Of course we laughed.

What she didn't realize was, we were not laughing with her; she was the joke. When she visited him for the weekend, she was our topic of conversation. We would read our notes from her aloud and laugh at every word she had falsely written. I felt extremely guilty. But since I never wanted to be in her shoes, I kept my mouth shut and forced a chuckle or smirk. What else could I do? At the time there seemed to be no other option. I was caught in my own trap.

Then she found us out. To this day none of us figured out how. She didn't say much, concealing her tears and slowly backing out of our circle. She made other friends and had little to do with us for the rest of the year. She appeared happier, but when I looked into her coffee-colored eyes, I think I saw her sorrow. I always wanted to reach out, to apologize, to do something. I realized that I had hurt her as much as everyone else, and she had every right not to listen to a word I said.

I had taken the easy way out by being a follower and have vowed never to do that again. My "friends" are all going to the same college and as tempting as that might be, I feel that going away and starting over is the better choice.

We still all continue to spend weekends together, but we are one person short and have one less topic to discuss. I watch her with new friends and know she is better off. If I had just reached out, maybe she wouldn't have gotten so hurt. When I saw her backing away, I didn't realize that it was I who was trapped and that she was the lucky one. She was given another chance. That is what I am searching for now. ▣

Seeing My Brother

by Maritess A. Reusch

Finally, it's Saturday. I can't wait until tonight when I visit my brother, Matt. He's in a "facility," which is just a polite way to say he's in jail. Minors can only visit on weekends. I can't believe he's in there. It's so hard to accept everything that's happened.

Last month Matt and a friend decided to steal a car. Somehow they got the keys and took it. Unfortunately, they crashed when his friend swerved to miss hitting a dog. Luckily, no one was hurt, but they were definitely caught.

Matt's trial is next week. He's charged with possession of a stolen vehicle. They couldn't charge him with auto theft because he wasn't driving. We think that he'll get probation and have to pay for the car. He'll probably be working it off until he's thirty. I don't know what kind of job he can get since he dropped out of high school. I think my dad is going to get him a job where he works.

It seems like I'm the only one learning from Matt's mistakes. He did whatever he wanted, whenever he wanted, no matter how much he was punished. Maybe this experience will help him realize all he's done.

Some family members and friends say Matt has no

brain; others feel he has the common sense of a goat. I don't believe that, though. Matt is incredibly smart—give him a math problem and he'll solve it. He even helps me with my homework when I ask (maybe beg is more like it). I think he was just bored with school.

It's really hard on my parents, especially my mom. Sometimes in the morning when she's in the shower, I hear her crying. I hear every sniffle and whimper over the water. My heart is just dying for her. I run into my room and cry like there's no tomorrow. Sometimes I think having no tomorrow would be a mixed blessing. I wouldn't have to listen to her cry and beg God to help her son. I wouldn't have to be strong for her.

I remember the one time I did break down in front of her. She started to cry so hard, harder than I'd ever thought possible. She started to say things like I need to be strong for her and I'm all she has left. It made me feel guilty and ashamed. After all, Mom is the one who carried him for nine months and raised him. I can't imagine how it all feels to her.

My dad deals with this very differently. He was raised at a time when a man crying was a sign of weakness. Dad reacted the only way he knew how—with anger. He didn't hit anyone; he just kept talking about how none of his kids could have acted so stupid and not have something wrong with their head. He repeated over and over that he wanted Matt to be evaluated. Dad was a hell-raiser when he was a teenager, too. Maybe he didn't do anything this major, but still. Dad had a job when he dropped out of high school. Matt doesn't. Is this stuff genetic?

Matt's friends still call. They think it's a joke, like

nothing bad could ever happen to one of their friends. I wonder how they think we feel. That's what I used to think until my mom came to me crying and mumbling that Matt was in jail. I just stood there stunned with Mom hanging onto me sobbing her heart out. She was crying so hard her whole body shook. I thought that only happened in the movies.

My friends, even my boyfriend, heard about it and asked me all kinds of questions. I tried to make it into a joke and not show my emotions. My boyfriend saw right through me. Later, when we were alone, he asked me how I really felt. I broke down. He put his arms around me and whispered that it'd all be okay. He chanted it like a sacred prayer. I had finally found a shoulder to cry on, a safe haven to run to, an anchor in the emotional storm I was going through. I just let everything out. I don't know how long I cried, but it felt good.

I dealt with everything better after that. I don't let it build up inside me. I call my boyfriend and talk. I hate the uncertainty of not knowing what's going to happen next, but life goes on and I deal. That's all you really can do. Well, that—and be there for my mom and Matt.

Right now I just pray that Matt will change. Maybe if he knew what everyone else was going through, he would. He just needs to realize that his actions affect other people, especially those who love him.

You know what? I still love him. How can I not? He's always going to be my brother and I'll always be his sister. That's never going to change. Neither is the fact that I will always be there for him and help him when he needs it.

The only good thing about all this is that Mom knows where Matt is. Maybe she can rest easier knowing he's alive, not dead or in danger, even though jail wasn't the alternative she was looking for.

Whoa, it's 6:30 P.M. I need to get ready. Where's Mom? She should be here by now. What should I say to Matt? I hope I won't cry. It'll be hard enough. 🔳

4 Ideal Portraits

Photo by Denise Ankel

Dear Amy

by Amybeth Gardner

In life, there are moments when we, as human beings living in a world that sometimes seems superficial, are touched by rays of hope. It's easy to forget that while society seems to be corrupt and we are struggling to become the best we can, there are good, unselfish people out there willing to give what they have in order to enrich the lives of others.

Adolescence is one of the most insecure periods of life, but I was always more than just insecure. I was riddled with low self-esteem but constantly trying to outdo myself. I was seldom proud and always reluctant to accept compliments. Sometimes, however, what I did surprised me with its courageousness, like that rainy Saturday afternoon when I wrote the letter I had been meaning to send for nine years.

Although many refuse to admit it, we all have idols. If I could take small qualities from certain people—writers, singers, musicians, poets—and combine them to form myself, I would be happy with who I am. Perhaps by writing this letter I could achieve some aspect of that goal.

I wanted to know her secrets: why she was such a good lyricist; what made her so articulate and candid at times but relentlessly private at others; how she could have survived the turmoil of the music business since the early seventies. While I wondered, I also respected her and appreciated her music. It was her words I could always relate to, her instrumentals that helped me study. It was often frustrating because she was never a favorite with my friends. But they accepted my love of her music and, except for occasionally teasing me, they understood why I was moved by it.

Mailing the letter was perhaps one of the bravest things I have ever done; not only did I tell her everything about myself, but I enclosed some of my most personal poems and watched fearfully as the mailman drove away, my dreams trapped in his truck. I knew I would most likely not hear from her, or at the very most, I expected some fan-club information, but what I received in the mail two weeks later shocked me and completely changed my outlook on life.

It was the kind of envelope that comes with personal stationery—small, with her return address stamped on the back. Tearing it open, I could only read the first line: *Dear Amy . . .*

The words were jumbled together and I realized that not only had she acknowledged my letter, but she had written by hand to tell me I had touched her deeply, even though she was in the midst of promoting a brand-new album.

My poems were good, she said, but if I could be a bit looser, letting the creative side come forth, I would be better. She closed the letter with, *Let me know . . . Love, Carly.*

My first instinct was to follow her directions

completely, writing freely, whatever came into my mind, and I immediately sent these thoughts to her, hoping for another response. I didn't realize what I was asking until I received another letter exactly one week later. She had not only torn through my thoughts, but rewritten them in a wonderfully poetic format, instructing me on how to improve, congratulating me for trying.

I became greedy. I wanted her to read everything I had ever written. I didn't realize how busy she was, and I again took advantage of her generosity by sending another poem, asking to be helped with her editing techniques. My perceptions were so cluttered; I hadn't taken the time to sit down and read what she had said as if she were a teacher and not a superstar singer/songwriter.

The third and final letter I received was much like the second: she had made so many corrections that her suggestions were written in the thin margins, taking up the entire page. She then went on to rewrite what I had written, giving me some of the best suggestions I had ever had. My disappointment followed when she explained that her editing had taken an hour, and she would not have that kind of free time anymore. But she knew I was getting better and I just needed to believe in myself.

I know you can do it, she wrote. *You're going to be really good . . . take these lessons, I hope you can learn from them on your own . . . Love, Carly.*

When the letters stopped, I sat down and read all of them over and over. When I finally absorbed what she had said, it all became clear to me. I wrote her a farewell thank-you letter and never heard from her again. Maybe her way of believing in me was not letting me become dependent on her and forcing me to have more faith in myself. I'll never know how to thank her for such a wonderful realization.

Few people today would have done what she did. During the four weeks we wrote letters, I admired her on talk shows and late-night shows, as well as television specials and radio programs, so I knew her time was scarce.

Soon after she wrote me, my name probably became a foggy memory to her, if that at all; but I will always remember her generosity, kindness and honesty. Thank you, Carly Simon, for proving to me that there is hope out there, and thank you for giving some of it to me. ◎

Photo by Aaron Schwartz

Meeting Superman

by Meredith Lee Ritchie

I called him Clark Kent. He was built just like him, tall and muscular with dark hair. Unshaven and obviously exhausted from a long day's work, Clark Kent entered Stewart's Root Beer, where I worked as the almighty take-out cashier. His clothes were dirty and his hands weathered from years of hard labor. I hardly noticed him as he shuffled through the fingerprint-smeared door.

It was August, the time of year when anyone would die for a cool drink and a fan blowing in her face. It was definitely not a time for hard labor, and the man's sad, weary expression showed his day had not been good. I had instant empathy for Clark Kent.

I had already been working for three hours that humid Saturday afternoon. I was dying to jog the two blocks to the beach and cool off in the greenish-blue waters of the ocean. The air conditioning had broken the night before and, adding to the heat, the tiny restaurant was packed. Everyone was edgy; everyone wanted what they wanted and there was no stopping them. My coworkers were about to wring each others' necks and the customers were rude, impatient and dissatisfied. I was going insane.

Clark Kent waited silently at the end of the take-out

line while everyone in front of him whined, moaned, pouted and yelled. Not once did he say a word about how long he'd been waiting. After twenty minutes of me pushing buttons, taking money and getting sodas, it was his turn to order.

"Welcome to Stewart's. How may I help you?" I asked mechanically, without lifting my eyes from the computer keys. Silence. I looked up and there stood Clark Kent. Despite his dingy appearance, he had the most beautiful green eyes and a childish smile.

"What can I get you, sir?" I was getting impatient. Someone behind him was already making a wisecrack. One more second of this nonsense and I was going to burst.

"Sir?" I asked again, more impatiently.

"Good morning. What's your name, dear?" he asked in a gentle voice.

"Meredith," I stuttered, dumbfounded.

"Good morning, Meredith. I'm not too hungry and I don't really like root beer," he paused. "But as I was walking by, I saw you working your tail off to please these people, and not one making an effort to please you. I thought you might need a pinch of sun to brighten your day."

I looked at him, and a single tear ran down my face. He was dirty, exhausted, worn, and my hero. For some-one who seemed to have lost so much, there was still so much for him to give. Without a thought of himself, he went out of his way to show me he cared. It is not every day that you meet someone like Clark Kent. The love he showed me in that one smile and those few words kept me on a natural high for the rest of the summer.

From the bottom of my soul, I thank you, Clark Kent. You are not Superman, but you very well could have been. You do not move mountains, catch evil villains or fly through the sky, but you are a hero just the same. Wherever you are, you moved mountains in my life, you caught the evil villain in my soul, and you fly still through my dreams from time to time. ▣

More Than a Teacher

by Melissa Robin Fadul

I don't know when I realized she was a genius, but when I did, something hit me—she's someone who answers those questions you thought had no answers.

Mrs. Feldberg isn't your average teacher. She doesn't care for normalcy, but somehow makes time for everything. Modesty, being too modest, is her greatest fault. She always knows what to say, and her little tidbits mean the most. Sometimes spurts of rebelliousness come alive, like when she says, "Don't justify who you are; let it be." She accepts what is there, but always looks to change what doesn't seem right. Reading poetry, the words dance off the pages for her—or through a tiny statement, she changes everything.

Mrs. Feldberg teaches English—love, anguish, sorrow and hope all rolled into one. I first met her in tenth grade. She spent the whole period telling us about her first days of school. From that moment I knew I had found a four-leaf clover in a forest. She taught me the importance of life through *To Kill a Mockingbird,* acceptance of one another through *Black Boy*—and with poetry, she has helped me find myself.

When she read poetry, it was as if the whole world was

on hold. With a slight Irish accent and traditional Jewish demeanor, she took hold of that literature and turned it into a ray of sunlight beaming down on us, those buds, waiting to bloom. With her help, we did bloom.

I never before had a teacher who wanted me to explore the outskirts of life without a safety belt, but I did, and I survived. She put courage in me, and now uncharted waters seem charted.

She didn't teach the everyday way. We never had a goal, but every day was just a continuation of finding ourselves. In writing class, she asked us to put one word on our paper and from there connect the next word that came into our head. It ended up as a map to show us who we really are.

It's not only me who sees how she teaches, but every-one in school. We all know if we have a problem, we can talk to her. She acts less like a teacher and more like our conscience. At this age we can use it.

Humor never fails her, especially when she's reading my poetry. She sees things I don't see in my work, and it's at those moments when the truth shines through. We don't agree on a lot of things, but I know she always takes my opinions into account. In return, I always listen to what she has to say.

She once told us of an experience she had seeing New York City from a great distance. Describing the bridges lit at night as "necklaces," I said, shocked, "That's how our language should be used." It's very difficult to remember everything, but the one thing that sticks out the most in my mind is: Every time Mrs. Feldberg reads my poetry she says, "Thank you." She's thanking me. . . . ▣

Magical Hands

by Jason Li

Everyone's hands are different shapes and colors. My uncle's hands—a farmer's hands—are special because they do more work than many. He is my mother's oldest brother, so he inherited my grandfather's farm in China. He is a small man with a tough body. His hands are especially big and strong. Nobody wants to grasp them because they feel like something cutting into yours.

When you see his hands, you know how much work they do. They are colored black and their skin is the roughest part of his body. It looks like the bark of a tree, and the nails always hide some dust. His hands have deep lines and calluses. When I suggest he use some lotion, he always answers, "Next time, I put it." But he always forgets.

When I was a child in China, I thought his hands held magic. His hands could make wine, cook, carry me on his shoulders, throw me up and catch me, and bend big wooden stakes. When he did that, he always teased me, "If you are not doing good in school, I will bend you like this wood." I always escaped from him.

Whenever I saw him, his hands were holding tools and doing something. Sometimes I would follow him to the farm, which connects with the hills. Uncle would speak, "Go to another place and play. When I finish, I will call you." I'd run on the soft soil, and when I was tired I would sit and watch Uncle. He dashed the crop down; the wheat fell in the barrel like rain. I loved the sound of the wheat falling down. *Sai, sai, sai.* When he finished hitting the crops, he put the wheat in bags, then threw them on the rickshaw. He put me on the rickshaw, too. Then he pushed it home, his hands shining like gold under the afterglow.

Time shifted like water. When I was in ninth grade, my mother told me to work with my uncle because I failed the final test needed for me to continue in school. I went to his garden. He asked me to go to the other side and extract some sticks from the soil.

I thought it would be easy, but soon my hands felt burning pain. I looked and found a red point on my palm where a blister had appeared. The sun was hot and the garden was like an oven. I felt impatient and pretended to have a headache. He teased me, "Weak boy, rest under the trees."

I sat under an apple tree, watching Uncle. His hands moved like a machine, down and up. The sticks gathered on the ground like a hill. The sweat soaked his shirt. When he finished most of them, he sat beside me and asked, "You okay?" I said I was and watched his hands, saying, "Your hands are like metal." He smiled and replied, "When you work hard, even the needles can't hurt you. Come on, let's finish." I felt so ashamed when he clasped my shoulder because I had tried to fool him.

Through rain or winds, Uncle takes care of his crops.

He uses his hands to make his crops grow. He also gains people's respect. His hands might look ugly, but even gold cannot compare to them. I admire him for having the kind of hands that will never change, but will be strong and rough. ▣

Photo by Kelli Bollin

To Be Old Like Uma

by Susan DeBiasio

On the terrace with the old lady.
What wild irises, colored purple-brown!
Uma studied the ground for ladybugs;
she thought they were magnificent
like one would think a rare gem.
Summer's weak sighs combed through
that fine silvery hair, lopped to one side
of her skull and fashioned with a plastic
butterfly. I talked at her of things like
new babies and weddings and funerals,
and when she smiled at me it was politely.
I could not know—for I was young—
that faces bobbed in the snowy whipped clouds
or that delicate voices sifted through the trees
or that sweetly pink childhood
had found its way back to her,
bearing all its simple pleasures.
Uma's twisted lips puttered quietly,
and now and then a giggle would shake her
  ancient bones,
and I would be warmed with pity.
But for whom?

Clown

by Robert M. Stolper

We were all sitting expectantly in our seats when the music blared. It was a quick-paced circus tune filled with trumpets, horns and cymbals. The rich aroma of roasted peanuts and the buttery smell of fluffy popcorn wafted to our noses. Before us formed a Big Top, with white and red striped canvas, thick wooden poles stretching to the sky, and three shallow blue circles in the center. The lights dimmed until only a single spotlight emerged and, with a magnificent drum roll, the main attraction entered.

He stumbled into the room. Thick, mangy red hair grew wildly from his egg-shaped head. Two blue triangles lay below his eyes, and a large crimson ball stuck to his nose. A goofy white smile, outlined in red, adorned his floury face. He constantly tugged at the oversized yellow pants, fervently hoping the green suspenders would fulfill their duty. The tiny pink shirt clung to his chest and seemed to reach down past his knees where it turned into tight socks. And just as he was about to make it to center stage, his enormous red shoes slapped into each other and sent him tumbling head over heels.

The class was silent. This was not what we had expected our teacher to be like. This man seemed befuddled and bewildered, like some absentminded scientist. Some laughed and others immediately tuned out. I leaned forward in interest to watch this unexpected teacher. He appeared unsure of what to talk about; it almost seemed as if the students were running the class.

It was when I had almost given up on him, almost surrendered to the comical appearance, that he looked at me. I saw in those eyes an intelligence that surprised me. It was as if it were not we who were laughing at him, but he who was laughing at us. His amusement was not cruel, but affectionate. He knew what we thought and did not care.

That made me smile. ▣

Photo by Amanda J. Luzar

Breezy Companion

by Liz Qually

Being an only child in a small town can be a little lonely and boring at times. Ever since I can remember, I was always looking for a friend and something to do. The outdoors became a very important part of my life. The weather took on a personality. Hidden growths and underbrush became my exclusive hideaways. Of all the natural phenomena, the wind was my favorite and over time became my friend, like an old stuffed animal or clung-to doll.

The wind was alive with the world's mystical wisdom and a passion for life. The wind would whistle through the huge trees in the backyard. Like an understanding mother, the trees' trunks would tremble and the leaves would quiver and rustle with murmurs of consolation. That small whisper of comfort became my savior and my friend. I told my new friend every accomplishment, and he in turn would rock the trees until they swelled to a roar of thunderous applause. I would walk outside to the greeting of my screaming fans and take a bow. When I was sad, the wind would swirl around me like a hug or a pat on the back.

I took to the wind so much because it was larger than life and omniscient. I could interpret its whispering rustles any way I wanted. I would play games and try to guide the wind with my hand. I cannot tell you how many times I asked to fly and in turn the wind would tell me, like a shrewd mother, that I would have to wait. Of course, it was impossible to fly, but the wind's answer was easier to accept.

I asked the wind many questions, but I already knew the answers. I would confide in my alter ego like a beloved teddy bear. The wind would accept all my secrets and never judge me. He never told me a secret in return, but I accepted this, for the wind was so wise and all-powerful. You never questioned your best friend.

As I grew older, the wind became less of a friend and more of a release. I loved to run in the field with a cool breeze surrounding me. I would dance in the swirling mass of air. It was like swimming under water. There was no one around but the outdoors and me. The wind would block signs of civilization and blow the grass like a thick carpet. With the growing stresses of being a teenager, a day in the sun with bare feet seemed the only freedom that could relieve the tensions of the real world.

Slowly, my friend and I drifted apart. I had a busier life, and he was content to blow the trees without me.

Now I have no time to greet my old friend and barely see him anymore. My idol and conscience has slowly changed into the guise of a weather pattern who barely speaks to me. Now I have to rely on my own judgment completely and I have grown independent. I miss him, but also understand the long-ago friend who left . . . of course, every so often he peeks his head out at me and waves. ◙

Important Small Talk

by Urszula Paliwoda

Phones ring, buzzers sound, lights flash while white tennis shoes rush down the linoleum floor. Shrieking patients restrained to their beds startle visitors passing in the hall. Ann's second home, this hospital, with its white walls, exhausted nurses and new construction, needs volunteers to give patients personal contact. After a year of constant hospital stays, Ann feels the isolation and depression settle.

"I only have one brother left. I live alone in my apartment with no reason to leave my bed," said Ann when I returned with her water pitcher. This dismal statement doesn't represent her; she's full of life. Her spirit lives as a child's, but it's deep inside, under all the choking sorrows that overflow in her lap. The inner child can't speak, sing or dance, when everything around it decays.

After standing on my feet all day, I sit on the empty bed across from her. Inhaling seems second nature to me, but Ann struggles with violent coughs, wheezing for oxygen. A clear cord connects her to life. Thirty years of smoking have burned Ann's lungs into blackened ashes, causing emphysema. A machine-operated human, Ann breathes, excretes and digests food through tubes.

Initially, I feared spending my afternoon with this old

woman, since my grumbling stomach informed me of its hunger that needed satisfaction. I've spent many afternoons with patients who needed attention; even I'd appreciate someone listening to me if I was isolated in my room. Today, I wanted some peace and quiet with my food, but it didn't happen.

Ann tells me intimate details about her family history and her marriage. Unfortunately, she is now a lonely widow with only one brother who lives nearby. She spends her days in her apartment, never leaving. Her groceries are delivered, doctors make house calls, and her associates are dead. Sympathy fills my heart as tears fill my eyes, picturing Ann's frail body in her old apartment with no one. Ann smiles profusely in my presence, and I wonder how long it has been since she's enjoyed a simple conversation with anyone—who would spare the time?

In my four years, I have had many responsibilities as a hospital volunteer: giving visitors information, running from one department to another delivering mail, changing restriction information, feeding patients, answering questions and making "small talk" with them. Today's "small talk," however, reminded me how easily a person blends into the background. Ann thanked me over and over for spending that hour with her, sharing my time when the busy world had forgotten her. ▣

The Doc

by Linsey A. Stevens

I was born with congenital heart defects that have, over the years, required three open-heart operations and multiple hospital stays. Sadly, for most children, hospitals are scary places filled with strangers and pain. For me, it was just the opposite.

I never feared the hospital. In fact, I looked forward to it. Part of these positive feelings may stem from my adventurous personality, though I doubt it. I know my views were positively affected by the people who always made me feel comfortable, no matter what my surroundings. They were a big part of my life and my heroes.

One person who greatly affected my view of hospitals, and even life, is Dr. Mark Boucek. He was my cardiologist until I was eight years old. I can remember his kind and cheerful way that always brought a smile to my face. He went the extra mile to make me feel comfortable whenever I was in the hospital.

I vividly remember one particular day. The room was dim, but the Sesame Street wallpaper cheered up the sterile feel of the Intensive Care Unit. The room was silent, except for the constant beeping of patients' heart monitors and a television far in the distance. The nurse brought my lunch, but it was difficult to eat with just my left hand. I kept fumbling with my silverware and she helped me get started. After I finished, I opened a can of orange soda. I wondered where my mom was; she was usually around. I hoped she would come; I was bored with no one to talk to.

Suddenly, the heavy silence was broken with laughing and chatting out in the hall. I wondered who it was, and my question was answered when Dr. Boucek and an entourage of others entered the ICU. I cheered up immediately when I saw him. He was the nicest man I knew and was very funny, too. Dr. Boucek carried a clipboard and wore a big grin.

"So, how's my patient feeling today?" he asked in an enthusiastic voice.

"Oh, I'm fine," I replied and added, "but it's hard to eat because my IV is on my right hand. I'm not used to using my left hand for this kind of stuff."

"Well, that is too bad we put the IV in your right hand. Next time we'll make sure we put it in your left," he answered in a concerned tone. He then proceeded to check my charts and machines while he and the others consulted with my nurse. He asked me a few questions and I answered as best I could. Mostly, I smiled at all his attention as I fussed with my soda.

Just when I thought Dr. Boucek was leaving, he pulled a very large syringe from his coat pocket. I broke into a smile and tried to cover my face with my arms; this was one syringe I loved. As the group headed out the door, Dr. Boucek lagged behind and took aim with the syringe. A jet of water squirted from it and hit me squarely in the face. I shook the water off and laughed as he gave a final wave and smile before he left.

Suddenly, I realized what a miracle worker Dr. Boucek was. Not only did he treat my physical problems, but he made a seven-year-old feel completely comfortable in a hospital ICU. I was hooked up to machines and couldn't move from my bed, but when he was around, none of that mattered.

Although I only have a few memories of him because I was so young, I remember now how he taught me to laugh in situations that seemed somber and disappointing. He showed me that if you take a little time to help someone, it can affect their life in ways you might never realize. He showed me what it is like to be the everyday hero for someone who needs a little extra help. ◙

One Special Aunt

by Dwayne J. Price

Brave, smart, compassionate and loving are just a few words that describe my hero. No, she isn't a movie star or a musical legend, and hasn't even heard of Third Eye Blind, but she is, in every respect, amazing.

She is my aunt, Anna Louise. She treats everyone with respect and does everything she can to help others. From volunteering at church to making sure none of her nieces and nephews ever miss an appointment, practice or rehearsal, she always has time to do things for others.

Anna Louise has inspired me since I was small, always pushing me to try new things and do my best. She introduced me to singing when I was only five by enrolling me in our church's youth choir. Every Wednesday evening for six years she would pick me up for choir practice. Afterward we would get ice-cream cones and have a contest to see who still had theirs by the time we got back to my house.

She took me to plays at a local theater. When I was nine I told her how much I enjoyed them, and she suggested I audition for the upcoming production of "The Sound of Music." I did and got the part of Kurt von Trapp. Almost every night I had two-hour rehearsals, and

Aunt Anna Louise would drive me seventy-two miles because she knew how much I enjoyed acting.

Acts like this make me realize how much she loves me and how much joy she gets from seeing me happy. I have been in two other plays and she once again was my transportation. I plan to major in music and minor in acting when I go to college.

Aunt Anna Louise has always helped me do activities she knew I would love. She sent me to camp in third grade. Now I am a counselor because I want other children to love camp and have as much fun as I did. In sixth grade I wanted to be in band, but my parents couldn't afford to rent an instrument. Anna Louise bought my first flute, and for my last birthday bought me a new one.

To Anna Louise, everything happens for a reason, and the unexplainable, no matter how horrible, has a purpose. Two years ago her husband, Butch, had a sore on his foot that would not go away. A doctor said he had blood poisoning and hospitalized him on a Thursday. We visited him Saturday and he was so weak he could barely move. The next morning the hospital called to tell us he was in Intensive Care and slipping away. We rushed to the hospital, but were too late. As the doctor came to talk to us, I let out wails and uncontrollable sobs while Aunt Anna Louise maintained her composure and talked to the doctor. I have no idea how she was so brave, but at that moment I knew she was the most courageous person on Earth and that I wanted to be like her.

Uncle Butch died on Father's Day, the day I was supposed to leave for church camp. I thought I needed to stay home and help my aunt, but she insisted I go. She knows me too well; if I'd stayed I would have broken down at his funeral and wouldn't have been able to control myself.

My Aunt Anna Louise may not be famous or have written an award-winning novel, but that doesn't matter to me. In my eyes she is the most wonderful person in the world. I love her and hope that when I have nieces and nephews, I can be as much of an inspiration to them as she has been to me. ▣

Photo by Sabine Selvais

Once

by Nicole C. Corvey

He stands
Too close to the television
Jingling the change
In his pockets
In deep thought
He bites his tongue

His presence brings a sort of comfort
I would never know again
His step is so strong
And sure
I never knew
It could falter
You could never tell
He wouldn't live forever

I didn't know I had a war hero in my home
All I knew was that
I had a protector,
Ally,
Friend,
And grandpa once

Once upon a time

5 Family Events

Photo by Stephen Siperstein

Fake

by Bonnie Tamarin

My mother trusted me when I told her I didn't smoke, even after she found a pack of cigarettes in my desk drawer. I didn't trust her when she said that the only reason she was going through my desk was to find some tape.

She didn't get mad when I broke my second contact lens in six weeks. She didn't even question me when I told her I borrowed her favorite white sweater and spilled red nail polish on it. My mother just smiled her usual, lopsided smile and forgave me. But, it took me two weeks before I forgave her for not buying the brand of wheat bread I preferred. I also found it unforgivable when she made me listen to her hillbilly rock music station, when we could have been listening to INXS. I'm still convinced that she insisted I wear a helmet to all those ice-skating parties when I was six just to make me look like a fool. I'll never forget the way people crowded around me asking why I was wearing a helmet. I would just tell them the truth: My mother made me.

For all these years I've been wishing my mother didn't do all the things she did. That was before I met Valerie. It was her first summer at camp, while it was everyone else's sixth. Her hair was blonde with black roots and she had a scar that ran across her forehead.

At night, everyone would sit in a circle and talk about everything. We would share anecdotes about boys, our parents and friends. I told my famous story about how I had tried to dye my hair blonde, but my mother wouldn't let me because she didn't want me to become "fake." Everyone giggled at my exaggerated story except Valerie. She just ran her fingers through her bleached hair and smiled. When it was time for her story, she began to rub the scar on her forehead nervously. I couldn't take it any longer; I just had to ask how she got that scar. I blurted out my question, which was returned with a deep stare from Valerie's brown eyes.

"I was ice skating and . . ."

I didn't even hear the end of her story. I just smiled to myself as I remembered those ice-skating parties. Everyone would give me such harsh looks as tears ran down my face. I also remembered staring in the mirror at my boring brown hair, listening to my mother tell me, "At least you're not 'fake.'" ▣

My New Beginning

by Martha Collins

When I was two years old, I was placed in a foster home. From that day, until a few years ago, I lived in four foster homes. When I was ten, I went to live with the Johnsons. It was a Sunday and rather chilly in the beginning of December. I was seated in a church pew listening to the sermon, when I realized I was fidgeting. I was scared about going to a new Sunday school class.

Later as I crept into the Sunday school room for fourth-graders, I noticed a beautiful woman with shiny, light-brown hair and dazzling blue eyes. I wondered if she would be my teacher. She introduced herself as Cheryl and asked us to read from a book. While we read, she tiptoed around the table, leaving the scent of wildflowers trailing behind her.

On the last day of class that year, I approached Cheryl and said, "I may not be back next year and wanted to thank you. You have been a wonderful teacher and friend." She gazed at me and asked, "Why don't you think you will be back?" I explained, "I might be getting adopted and if I do, I will be living in another city."

On my birthday, July 11, I had a party. Cheryl and her husband, Steve, came since they were friends of my foster family. The adoption process had already begun—without my knowledge. In August, my foster mom told me I would soon be adopted. She couldn't say by whom, though. As I was getting into bed, I began to cry. I told my foster sister I was terrified about the next day. I didn't want to end up with a family who didn't care about me. She got my foster mom, who talked to me and made up a game where I would guess who my adoptive parents were. She would not tell me, but gave me clues. I kept guessing until she said it was time to go to sleep—tomorrow would be a very emotional day.

I went to sleep both happy and excited. The next day, I had a meeting with my adoption worker. Finally, the big moment arrived and I was finally told who my new parents would be . . . Steve and Cheryl! I went crazy, I was so happy. I knew and trusted them, and was friends with them, too! Later that night I called them. Cheryl answered and I said, "Hi, Mom!" We talked for a little bit and then I talked to Steve.

My visits began the following week when I spent the weekend with them! I met my sister, their biological daughter, Lisa and her fiancé, Brian, my new grandparents, aunt, uncle and cousin. Finally, later that month, I moved in. Their home was so cozy and warm I felt I had already lived with them forever. When Cheryl gave me a hug that night, I felt warm and loved. Then Steve came in, leaned over my new bed and also gave me a hug. I was so happy I felt like I could just float up to heaven.

When I woke the next morning, we packed and left for Wisconsin Dells. We spent the weekend going on rides, eating and having a lot of fun. At the hotel we all decided to go swimming, and as I was trying to get Steve's attention, I yelled "Dad!" That was the first time I had called him that. He was overjoyed! On the way home I called them Mom and Dad every time I wanted their attention. This is a time neither Mom, Dad nor I will ever forget!

The following spring we went to court, stood in front of a judge and became a family. The judge asked me if I wanted to be adopted by them. I said in a very timid but enthusiastic voice, "Yes." She asked them if they were sure. Together, and very excitedly, they said, "Yes!" When I heard that gavel hit, it was music to my ears! She had just pronounced us a family! The adoption was final. I was so happy! My new mom, dad and I gave each other a great big hug.

Since that day we have grown closer together. I was in Lisa and Brian's wedding and have become happier every day. I wish every child in foster care could find the new beginning I did. ◙

Gram

by Susan DeBiasio

At eighty-four, the old girl's soul
is ripe and tart like wine,
filling her dank and musty body
like a forgotten cellar.
Sitting in a chewed blue armchair all day
makes her a tight wad of nerves.
Her wild eyes dance maniacally behind useless panes;
her flaming tongue spurts senseless, spicy words
at people passing.
She is a queen, that little dragon lady,
a queen on a threadbare throne.
But that suits me just fine;
to me she's as darling as a restless child
watching a wet, white snowfall
smother the playground in December.

My Unknown Grandfather

by Selma Siddiqui

We share many things: deep brown eyes, a big nose, a strong but small build. But, mainly, we share an independence, a need for all things wild, natural and beautiful. We share a craving for the richness of life with its timeless traditions and bold new frontiers. We are one person of two different times; one soul of two bodies; two minds of one heart. My grandfather and I bear such an uncanny similarity that it boggles my mind to think I never knew him, never once touched his face, held his hand or took a long, leisurely walk by his side.

My grandfather was a locomotive engineer in Pakistan in the 1950s. He used to drive steam engines throughout the unending desert that surrounded the nation of brown and brilliant people. I see him in my mind, at peace in the small confines of the engine room, stoking coal in the boiler, driving the train, his gaze forever bound to the thick brown sand that encompassed him. He was a person of brute strength, able to carry heavy shovels of coal; he was a person of mental strength, able to stand for hours, alone, in a small steel box, with endless desert flowing past his fingertips while firmly holding the steering bar.

He was a strong individual, my grandfather, never afraid to be alone. In addition to driving the train, Grandfather loved to take walks, miles long, by himself, into the unforgiving desert. With each footstep, the burning sand would glide gently over his thin sandals to tickle the soles of his feet, but little would he notice, for his skin was rough and callused. Though my grandfather seemed a solitary man, he had a softer side, a tender, loving side, a side utterly bewildering to those who only saw the firm, stolid facade he proudly wore.

His one and only hobby was photography. It was the solitary pastime of a solitary man. Out into his desert he would go, camera in hand, ready to take the pictures that spoke in a rhapsody of rhyme to the beholder's eye, for he knew well that language would never say what his pictures could.

Grandfather was a unique man, and he took great pride in that. His clothes were most interesting: his pants cut for a gorilla, and his shirts large enough to hold his three sons. As for style, a rainbow of color seeped over every inch of fabric, leaving the world bathed in his brightness.

And somehow, without ever knowing him, I am like him. Even though I don't drive a steam engine, his solitary manner seems to coincide perfectly with mine. I love to be alone, grabbing the opportunity whenever it presents itself. Although I am without an endless desert, I walk alone for miles, with the buzz of traffic filling my ears. The desolate mind-set Grandfather kept, I somehow borrow from him.

But it's style we share—being unlike anyone else is

part of both our characters. His color and style seep into my own gorilla-sized pants, and his brightness has bathed my world. The rainbow of color is slowly gliding over me, stopping only long enough to grace me with his style.

My grandfather had so many nooks and crannies in his character; he was a puzzle of a life, a man not meant to be understood but enjoyed like a gentle breeze caressing the senses. And, though I didn't try at first, with each passing day I want more and more to be like the man who died ten years before my birth. The puzzle of a life that he was, I wish somehow to be a part of, to be like the man whose life was enjoyed by all who knew him. Perhaps by encompassing part of his character, I can somehow meet the man I will never know and take a long, leisurely walk by his side. ◙

Photo by Kristen Bonacorso

The Baby-Sitter's Promise

by Shana Onigman

I had only baby-sat for my half-brother, Scott, once or twice, even though he was three months old. I had spent a lot of time around him, though, and knew how to care for him, so my dad was pretty comfortable letting me watch him for two hours while he went to the airport to pick up my step-mother. I was all right with it, too, since Scott was an unusually happy baby who would smile at anything and rarely cried.

"You know where the emergency phone numbers are," he said, "and he shouldn't have to eat until 6:30 P.M., but we'll be home by then, and . . ."

"Dad, you're treating me like a new baby-sitter," I interrupted rather disgustedly. "I've baby-sat for him before. I know what to do."

Or so it appeared the first fifteen minutes we were all there. Scott smiled and cooed at me like his usual self— until, of course, with the perfect timing that all babies have—Dad's cab pulled up. Then, Scott decided to scream.

"Is he okay?" Dad called from the other room, as he got ready.

"I don't know," I shouted uneasily over the baby's

wailing screams. "Does he need to be changed or eat?" *It is probably the latter,* I thought. Scott was a big baby; in fact, he was off the chart. He was always eating, and I feared he was doomed to become a football player.

Dad stopped on his way out the door. "I just changed him, and he shouldn't have to eat yet, unless he's planning on gaining another ten pounds by next week." Dad smiled, secretly proud of his monstrous son. "Try to get him to go to sleep. I'm leaving."

Scott screamed all the louder, his mouth wide open, the shrillest noise he could muster filling the room. I sang to him, tried to burp him, and even reduced myself to making faces at him, but he couldn't see me since his eyes were squeezed shut in his mottled, red face. My eardrums were taking a severe beating.

I tried to change him, but his volume somehow increased. I wondered if the neighbors could hear, and if any of them had called the police to report an infanticide yet. Begging him to be quiet, I plugged his mouth with a pacifier. He screamed more.

Apparently, I did not have the patience of the average mother who could put up with this sort of madness for days on end. After half an hour of his nonstop crying, I found that crying, like yawning and hiccups, is contagious, and soon tears of frustration and exasperation were running down my face.

His crying wouldn't have bothered me so much if he had been the type of baby who cried a lot, but he wasn't; he always smiled. From the grating shrieks, it sounded like he was in pain, but I had no idea how he could be. I wondered how teenage mothers dealt with their babies, and with a sudden shock I realized that he could have been mine. We both continued crying: he for whatever was wrong with him, and I for those in worse situations than me, and for the sad and painful demise of my eardrums.

Scott's screams showed no sign of letting up and so I decided that he had to be hungry, or at least thirsty. Praying, I tried to give him some water. After a few futile minutes, he finally let out a belch so loud that it probably would have impressed a five-hundred-pound truck driver. I held my breath: *Was he going to be quiet?* No, wishful thinking. The screams resumed, and I tried singing to him through my own tears. No, he would have none of that either. Finally, I just hugged him and begged him to quiet down, and mercifully he did, after totally ruining any nerves I might have had left and my irrational desire to have children when I grew up.

I gently laid him down in his crib, mentally daring him to open even one eye. Thankfully he didn't, and I leaned over the edge of his crib.

"Scottie," I whispered to the sleeping baby, so angelic now that he was unconscious, "I promise I will take care of you until I go to college, but I will never, ever have children of my own. You can quote me on that."

Scott opened his eyes. I cringed, expecting him to start bawling again. Instead, he gave me a toothless grin, closed his eyes and went back to sleep. ▣

A Song Called "Butterfly Kisses"

by Michele Sampson

Plop! I dropped my purple dance bag that was overflowing with tap shoes, toe shoes, tights, leg warmers and all my other dance equipment. Next came the book bag off my back and my overweight leather jacket. After placing my glasses on the table and rubbing the pain in my shoulder where my dance bag had been, I went to tell my mom and dad that I had arrived home safely and kiss them good night.

I leaned over the blue comforter my dad was cuddled under to give him a kiss, but instead, he pulled my cheek close to his face and blinked his eyes so that his eyelashes tickled my face. I honestly thought he had lost his mind and wondered what in the world he was doing. He told me he was giving me a butterfly kiss. I just stared at him. He explained by telling me about a song he heard on the radio called "Butterfly Kisses." When he heard it, it reminded him of me.

That Sunday, right after church, I pulled my hair into a ponytail, jumped into a pair of gray sweats and removed my makeup. I was just about to make my mark on the beige couch in front of the television when my dad asked me if I would go to the store with him. Why not? He said I could drive.

Dads are great to go shopping with. Anything you put in the basket is all right with them. My dad is no exception. I think we ended up with four types of ice cream (vanilla, chocolate, coffee and butter pecan), a cake, cookies and the bread we originally went to get.

With brown bags covering the back seat, we were driving home when my dad said, "That's it . . . turn up the radio." "Butterfly Kisses" was playing.

I listened to the words and thought, *My dad said this reminds him of me.* Bob Carlisle, the singer and songwriter, told the story of the relationship with his daughter, and his memories of her growing from a young girl to her wedding day. What touched me the most was that the song suggested that the father must have done something great to deserve his daughter. Tears began to spill from my eyes. I tried to hide them from my father, but my nose started running, too, and my glasses were fogging up. He said, "Yeah, I know," and I realized he was crying, too.

I never felt as close to my father as I did that day. I love him very much, but like any teenage girl, I know I can be tough to live with. Every once in a while I try to remind myself of how I felt with my dad that day in the car, because it felt good. I look forward to the day I feel that close to him again—probably on my wedding day, when I dance with him to "Butterfly Kisses." ▣

Jukebox

by Rachel Mitchem

he redundant singing of an alarm clock awakens most people with an ear-piercing, rhythmic bleep creeping up on you, destroying the most pleasant dreams and even the most serene minds. In my house it's different. Instead of that steady blare agitating my entire body, I have my very own jukebox. In a way it's broken: The buttons don't work and you can't choose to listen to song number 678 and expect the Jackson Five to serenade you with "A, B, C." The tune is the same every time with different lyrics, a tired melody I learned in Bible school. Sometimes I find myself humming it while walking to class even after the jukebox has long since stopped. Of course, I am speaking not of a clock radio or even an out-of-style, brightly painted, metal box that switches records before my eyes—I am talking about my mother.

Her musical talent was left behind in high school along with her creativity, but certainly not her sense of humor. Each morning I thank God that I can be roused by a mere touch of the finger. If not, I too would have to put up with her excited craziness each morning. My eight-year-old brother, on the other hand, is not so lucky. He sleeps like one who passed out the night before and is afraid to wake up with a hangover. As an alternate way of lying down, he chooses to sprawl his entire corpse across the pillows with his legs askew in a pretzel position. He cannot be moved, not even by the loudest, most neurotic alarm clock. So he is anointed every morning with the sound of my mother's young-at-heart voice.

In an almost funny sort of way, she dances like an amateur ballerina through the hallway singing her famous Bible song: "Rise and Shine and give God the glory, glory. Children of their beds." These aren't the words, but it earns new endings each morning. Despite her crooning every morning and the fine display of stunning dance skills, my brother merely rolls off the pillows and hides himself unconsciously beneath the blankets. My mother is not easily discouraged and continues her antics more loudly, adding an occasional turn to her skip. Attempting to make up an entire verse, she sings the jingle over and over again.

Now completely awake, my brother throws his worn bear at her and buries his head in the pillow. He dares not face her because he knows that she will only mock his tousled hair and smother him with pillows. The jukebox persists with her weary song as my brother tries to return to a pleasant slumber. But since he has shown that he is indeed not dead, my mother begins to tickle him with all her might. His legs fly wildly about the bed dancing uncontrollably to the jukebox. His arms fly about her face as if trying to break the "glass" on the jukebox to silence it. But now his sleepiness has turned into laughter and he rolls over to smile at her bright face. She smiles back and kisses his forehead, telling him to get his lazy butt out of bed. While he gets dressed, my mother hums quietly the never-changing melody of her broken record collection. She has succeeded in her morning objective—even though we are already late. ▣

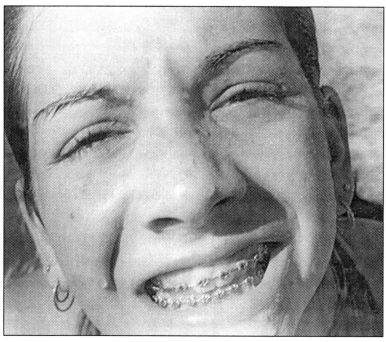

Photo by Nicole M. Gulla

Of Mothers and Daughters

by Linda Liu

A moment
suspended in midair
electric sparks passing through
bloodlines between us
My mother and I
sitting at the dinner table
stomachs full
Eat more—says She,
my daughter, You will grow
taller than me
stronger than me
away from me
I frown at her ignorance, how could She not know
She is in my laughter
the fat on my hips
my ambitions
the fear I have of spiders. She courses
through my veins
giving nourishment
bathing my organs in an Omnipotent Red River.

Portrait of Nick

by Shari Moore

Nick. A dent in my mask to remind me to never, ever put salt in his deodorant.

Nick. A notch left as a hint to never, ever take a mannequin's head, add a body dressed in exotic clothing and stuff it in his bed at night.

Nick. A scrape on my skin is a remembrance to never, ever wear his clothes or he'll rip my arm off.

Nick. A scratch; never, ever soak his toothbrush in substances unapproved by the health administration.

Nick. A gash to remember that I will never, ever again pour liquid soap over the dishes so the dishwasher overflows when it's his turn to do the dishes.

Nick. An incision to prompt me to never, ever spread toothpaste and shaving cream over his friends at night when he has a sleepover. Never again will I leave him with the evidence in his hands while his friends slumber, the shaving cream soaking into their pruned skin while the minty paste stabs at their nostrils.

Nick. Most important, a gouge that has scarred me for life. A brother who always understands. An ally I can always count on in an innocent game of snowball riot. A shield that makes sure no one picks on his little sis.

So, next time you ask, "Hey, is Nick Moore your

brother?" once more, grinning from ear to ear, I'll reply, "Yes."

Don't say, "I feel sorry for you" (even though you probably won't because you have some melodramatic crush on the poor guy) because I'll have to disagree.

Nick, the appalling.

Nick, the harrowing.

Nick, the insufferable. He's actually my quarry, my prey, my game.

He's Nick, seventeen and destined to die young from food poisoning or rotting skin, and all because of my mask of deception.

Nick. My brother, my victim, my friend. ◙

So Young

by Anna Isaacson

ose is dying. This thought was true and okay. I could see it lingering above everyone's heads. But my thoughts that followed brought guilt, guilt. Underneath the masks of solemnity, which my siblings and I all wore like uniforms, I didn't care. My life would not change when Rose was gone. I did feel sympathy, but more for my grandmother than for her mother who was beside us breathing heavily enough to make me shudder.

But no love. My own great-grandmother, my Oma, and nothing. And so guilt. Oma looked sickly, horrifying. I remember her veins that protruded from her skin un-naturally. And her fingers, the fingers she and my grand-mother and my father all had, with the distinctive curves at the ends—they were the same fingers that used to grip my hand eagerly whenever I saw her. But now the skin hung loosely from them and had no strength to grip when it was my turn to hold that terrifying hand.

But no, none of this repulsion, I had to reprimand myself. I was not to look away. I was to hold that hand, yes. Was this face right, now? But too false, my sister and brothers and I. Too false next to the real pain of our grandmother. Our grammy who had spent so much of

her time taking care of Oma with consistent dedication—
what was she feeling? Grammy who had survived the
Holocaust with Oma. Grammy who had been through so
much. I was bewildered by the sympathy I felt, but sympathy is only so deep. And my father now leaving the
room to, oh, can it be, to cry for a moment? What did he
feel? My mother, how long had she even known Oma?
But now, in the drama of the moments in that room,
what was Mom thinking? And my siblings, I could only
assume that their thoughts were similar to mine.

I thought of the few days my family had spent visiting
Oma and I was so ashamed of how it had been. The four
of us had hated every second of the visits and loved ourselves for the sacrifice we were making. And Oma was
always so happy to see us, though sometimes confusing
me with my sister and asking the same questions twice.
We were so polite, and what else could there be? She
was so old; we were so young. She loved us and we
were too small to love her back, as though we were far,
far away from her and dwarfed by the distance.

I wanted to take back my selfishness and make it up
to Oma. No, I could not instantly love her then, even
under the pressure of my own guilt. But I could take her
hand and thank her for loving me. I could sit beside her
and hope that she would recognize and perhaps understand me from behind the blinds of death. I imagined
that my presence would bring . . . what? Happiness?
Relief from pain? I was twelve, ignorant, yet confident.

But only twelve, only wrong, only naive? No, I cannot
have imagined what I felt then. Oma murmured as I was
holding her hand. I can't remember her face. But, oh,

there was the smallest sting of sadness, and even pain, and the gentlest quiver of recognition, yes. Oma knew I was there, or at least that someone was there. Someone she loved? Someone she loved? ◙

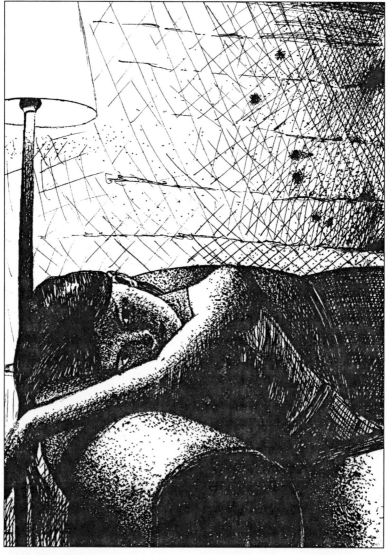

Art by Elisabeth Rametta

Oren

by Barney Schauble

It's a funny run you have, a sort of
skipping, trotting—laughing, too
as we play on the lawn
spotted summer sun and shadows
The grass is uneven, the net full of holes,
but we laugh together as we chase after the ball—
short legs racing to keep up
with longer, scarred ones.
Just the two of us
—brothers—
playing on a summer afternoon.

"Let's take a rest," you cry
so we sit, in the shade, and talk.
You're earnest, and also serious
in the childlike way you have of seeming
frighteningly old.
"I wish I was your age," you say
wistfully, looking at me, sideways.
You mean it, too—to you, seventeen
means tall and strong and capable
and ready for the "Nabal" Academy.

And I smile, and try to tell you, somehow
about the next twelve years
—about going to school, and playing sports,
and falling in love, and growing up—
that are so easy and fun and crazy
and difficult and full . . .
and how I wish I were four again,
and just beginning, carefree,
full of promise . . .
but you just laugh, so unconsciously
delighted with life
and ask me your questions about the world,
sure that I know the answers.

A Walk with Dad

by Marc R. Baron

My father and I are on our way to Walden Pond. I have never been there, but my father goes quite often. We sit silently in the car listening to his classical music station. The plush seat cradles me as we drive through suburban neighborhoods. Summer is thick in the air. The air conditioner cools as we drive.

We pull off the road onto a dirt path. My father pays the five-dollar parking fee. We walk from the parking lot and cross the street to the path that leads to Walden. I see people on bikes and little children escaping their parents' grasp, as I had once done with my father. We head down the path, stopping at a clearing to look at the pond.

"Well, what do you think?" my father asks, turning toward me.

I gaze out at the beauty before me and say, "Amazing."

Green water is circled by trees and sand. Typical, one might say, of every pond or lake. But this is different. I have seen many ponds and lakes, but nothing can touch what lies before me. It was not so much the physical beauty, but the emotional beauty. Walden dances along the edge of my being.

"Shall we walk around?"

"Sure, Dad, you lead the way."

So we start off. As we walk, I look around. Though the highway is only a few feet away, it feels as though we are in deep forest. Bugs and other little creatures crawl underfoot. The shade of the trees turns the hot day cool and comfortable.

We pass a young boy, nine or ten, fishing with his father. I turn to my father and think back to my younger years. My father is an intellectual, a thinker. When I was younger we would fight. Fight is not really the right word; we disagreed. I was young. He was old. He wanted me to be careful, respectful, neat and clean. All I wanted was to have fun. We could not find a middle ground. We did not scream at each other; we just stayed out of the other's way. Sure, he was still a dad and I was still a son, but we were not friends.

As I grew, I saw my father in a new light. I started to read and to think. I began to write poetry and enjoy learning. My father, who had been an English teacher, would read my writing and critique it. I respected his opinion and soon I respected him. I think he began to respect me.

"Careful, Marc!" my dad says, grabbing me from my thoughts as I trip over a root. He helps me gain my balance; I look at him. He's a very gentle, caring man. He loves me and wants the best for me. This is true of most dads, but how many show it? How many sons see this in their father's eyes? I never had. Walden Pond filters out the world. I can see my father up close, without distraction. I see a man, and a friend.

We conclude our walk around Walden Pond. I discovered my father today. As we watch tiny waves stroke the hot sand, I realize that a father's love is a lot like Walden Pond. It's always there; you just have to find it. My search was not for a place on a map, but a place in my heart. I had to love my father to see his love for me.

At the top of the path we turn and look back at Walden Pond.

"Amazing," my father comments, looking out onto the water.

I turn to him and say, "Yes, it is." 回

Always Sisters

by Alexis Bargelski

Sisters have a bond that lasts their entire lives. They share every moment from the most trivial to the most defining. My sister Tessa has always held a special place in my heart, and nothing that comes our way can change that.

My first memory of her sitting in a corner and drawing intently will never fade. My family had driven hours to the small, crowded orphanage to visit her. I can still see her chubby little face, concentrating on the masterpiece she was working on while other children raced around her. Adopting this three-year-old when I was seven was one of the best things that ever happened to me and my family.

Our first outing with her was on a sultry day during monsoon season in Seoul, South Korea. The scents of fresh rain and humid air still linger in my mind. Sitting across from the tiny girl in a cramped restaurant and watching her relish the Coke in front of her was at first uncomfortable. Worries of her not fitting into our family raced through my mind. *What if she doesn't like me? What if she is unhappy in her new home? When would she learn to speak English?* These thoughts seemed to be answered when, after polishing off two sodas, the little girl began to hold her stomach and whimper. My mother swooned over her and patted her back while my father frantically tried to find someone who could translate her rushed words. I knew at that moment everything would somehow work out in our new family.

Since that sticky afternoon, my sister and I have come to have a very close relationship. Our days of living overseas were filled with memories that only Tessa can understand. She reminisces with me about the business dinners with our dad aboard floating restaurants at dusk in Hong Kong. If I forget where we rode the baby elephants around the hotel, she reminds me that it was Thiamin. We laugh about the time I was bitten by a poisonous ant in Singapore; she had to hold my hand while the ancient doctor gave me a shot. We share memories of the extensive traveling we have been fortunate to experience.

We have also shared the bitter times that many teenagers endure. If one of us makes a wrong choice, the other is there to help. Tess and I have counted on each other many times to explain why one was suspiciously late coming home from the movies. Our secrets have to do with us growing into women, and sometimes parents cannot know the exact path we take. There is nothing I wouldn't do for my sister, and I know she feels the same. We used to make secret pacts, but we now have an unspoken loyalty that neither dares betray. Sometimes secrets and experiences create an unshakable bond that nothing else can. ◙

Just a Man

by Scott Nichols

You were just a man whose heart had turned to stone
Act fast, hit hard, take it like a man.
I was just a boy looking for your help.
Legs planted, palms open, one blow was all you gave.
The first hard hit was not enough
You had to break my jaw.
When years had passed and I grew up
You shoved my back against the wall.
Stand tall, don't run, I heard you say
But shattered glass was all I felt.

Even though your belt was black, you thought you
    were a man
But men have known from ancient times the lessons
    of the gods
That man is just a mortal soul whose place is
    firmly fixed
And when man thinks that he is god, the truth will
    never be.
Now I am a man, in spite of all your years
And standing tall against the world
The wind behind my back
I'll always know the man called dad
Was just a man whose heart had turned to stone.

Monumental Moments

Photo by Stephen Siperstein

Emily the Soccer Star

by Suzanne Timmons

ZZZZZZZZZ. The sound of my alarm clock was enough to make me jump. I turned over with a groan and stumbled out of bed. From the second my feet touched the carpet I could tell today was going to be another scorcher. I pulled on my hospital pants and white T-shirt. Although I tried to eat, the butterflies in my stomach won the battle and I settled for apple juice. Today I would begin my summer job. I was volunteering at the hospital. Although I had been excited when I had decided to work there, now I was very anxious about what I would be doing.

At the hospital I learned that most of my job would be taking patients to their rooms and doing other odd jobs. On Fridays, however, I would spend time in Pediatrics, visiting a child. The first few days passed quickly. By Friday, I had forgotten about my date on the Pediatrics floor. So when I was instructed to go to meet Emily, a leukemia patient, I tried to plaster a calm smile across my face, but inside I wanted to cry. Even with her lack of hair and an IV in her arm, she mustered the strength to smile and speak with me.

I soon learned that Emily was eight. She loved going to the beach and playing with dolls and had an older brother named Ryan. She was on the town soccer team and proudly informed me that she had scored more goals than anyone else on her team. With our incessant chatting, that first Friday very quickly came to an end.

When I told Emily I would be back in a week, she begged and pleaded for me to visit on Monday. I couldn't resist her toothless grin and so I "pinkie-swore" to be back after the weekend. It wasn't long before I was spending lunch breaks with Emily and leaving the hospital long after my shift had ended so I could spend time with her in the game room.

On days she felt strong enough, we played soccer, even though it was not allowed. It was hilarious to see the nurses turn their heads away, pretending not to notice when Emily's infamous and most prized possession, her black and white soccer ball, would fly through the air. On rare occasions, her illness would get the best of her and we couldn't play. On those days I would read her favorite books to her or we would play Barbies on her hospital bed. Once we even cut off Barbie's hair so that she could be Emily's twin.

I discovered many things that I admired about Emily. I was most impressed with her will to live. Not once did I see her shed a tear over the pain she must have been hiding behind those clear blue eyes. In addition, her constant optimism, along with her contagious laughter, made her unlike any eight-year-old I had ever met. She was wise beyond her years, and her incredible physical and emotional strength made her an inspiration.

Toward the middle of the summer, her "yuck days" (as she called them) began to outnumber her good ones. I remember one particular day when I arrived at Emily's room to find her in an unusual state: She was quiet and in a deep sleep. After talking to her mother I learned that Emily had been given her "life sentence"—she only had a couple of weeks left.

I went home that night with a pit in my stomach and a lump in my throat. I retreated to my room without dinner and cried for hours. I felt so helpless and would have given anything to take her pain away, but all I could do was hold her hand as she vomited from the medication being forced into her tiny body. Even more, I hated this disease that had wreaked havoc inside her and cut her life far too short. It was then that I decided to make the best of these weeks with Emily.

Even during her last few days, Emily brought joy into the lives of those around her. She laughed and giggled with everyone who visited, and she marveled at all the cards and stuffed animals she received.

One evening after dinner we played soccer—a special occasion because it was something she hadn't had the strength to do for quite a while. Ending the night with her favorite book, *Cinderella,* I once again "pinkie-swore" I would be back the next day for another round of soccer. She gave me the biggest hug that her frail body could muster.

The next day I sprinted down the corridor to see my favorite patient, but instead was greeted by her mother. Through tears she told me that Emily had passed away earlier in the morning. Her mother told me how wonderful I had made Emily's last few months, but that didn't ease my aching heart. Just as I was about to leave, her mother handed me an envelope with my name written in red crayon. I knew immediately it was Emily's handwriting because of the backwards "s" scribbled across the front. Opening the envelope in the car, I found a drawing of us playing soccer. On top was written "To my favorite soccer player." The tears that I so desperately tried to keep inside sprung from my eyes. It was at this moment that I realized I had been truly blessed by the presence of this amazing eight-year-old.

Even today when I start to forget, I take that folded drawing from my wallet, look at her tiny body clad in that teddy-bear hospital gown, and smile back at that toothless grin that taught me about life, love and friendship. 回

Opposites Attract

by Mark J. Murphy

I always thought I knew my type—the tall, blue-eyed, blonde-haired goddess that every-one is attracted to, basically the all-American Barbie doll.

Seventh grade not only meant a new school but new people, and that meant more Barbie dolls to pursue. I was excited, no, I was anxious to meet these beauties. You have to understand it was not a hormonal thing. I am a hopeless romantic with an obsession to love. I am in love with love, which is ironic considering I have never been in love, or at least I hadn't been to that point in my life.

There is only one person who stands out in my mind from seventh grade. She was my total opposite: a punk who wanted to be the center of attention. But there could be only one center of attention—and that was me. We butted heads from the moment we met. She was my rival, my competitor, and she was my challenger for being the class clown. Katelyn was the enemy in a war she just couldn't win. It was a relentless battle, a crusade with vin-dictive, harsh words, but one in which I thrived. We had a love-hate relationship . . . only without the love.

In eighth grade, Katelyn was just a memory. She was

not in any of my classes nor did I see her in the halls. Things change. People change. Time is the master of maturing. But an immature moment brought her back into my life—only now she was not the child I had once fought with.

In ninth grade, she was in most of my classes, so avoiding her was impossible. You see, this year, she and her rebel friends decided to throw food at lunch which got them assigned seats, and, of course, she was placed at my table. Why me? What did I do wrong to bring her back into my life? I never would have known she had turned into something bearable if it were not for her moment of childish behavior.

Could it be that immature, arrogant tomboy of a girl had grown into someone I could be friends with? Shocking, but yes. I never had such conversations and so much laughter as I did with her. She brought out a side in me I had long forgotten. Our relationship did a total one hundred and eighty degrees; we went from bashing each other to smiling and making faces. Through notes and many discussions, I learned Katelyn and I were two peas in a pod, one of a kind; we were more alike than I could have ever imagined.

So what had happened? She used to be so annoying, and I thought she looked like a puppy. I used to cringe at the thought of her. Now I only saw big, captivating, innocent green eyes and thin soft lips that formed the perfect smile. Even her cute little nose and charming childlike laugh made me think there was something about my old rival that was enchanting.

Was this a crush? Did I have feelings for her? Could I

be attracted to Katelyn? You bet, and it was not just infatuation. I was in love with her. It was the kind of love that makes you weak in the knees and puts butterflies in your stomach. I was stuck in a constant daydream and I always awoke with a smile. I found myself wondering, *Why Katelyn?* She was not the Barbie-doll goddess I thought I wanted. But I loved her. I loved her weird sense of style, her playfulness and her constant need to be right. I even loved how sometimes when she talked, she would blow spit bubbles.

It was the type of love that develops over a period. I remember the moment I realized my true feelings. It was right after French class and we always walked to our lockers. Since our lockers were in different directions we went our separate ways at the end of the hall. For some reason on this day, when we stopped to say good-bye, we pressed our heads together, looked into each other's eyes and smiled. Something had changed. In that moment when I thought we were going to kiss, I realized I was in love with her. I wanted to kiss her.

Could I tell her? Well, no, not right away. I did not say a word for months. In those months I spent every minute I could with her. I made sure she was the biggest part of my life. When I finally told her over the summer, she was surprised. I was heartbroken. She did not feel the same way. Later that year I told her again and this time she agreed to try dating. Those were my happiest moments.

However, our romantic relationship did not last. We were friends first; no, we were best friends. I loved her, and I still do. Having Katelyn as my best friend is all I need. I would not trade any of the time I've spent with her. When I look into my future I see her there. I cannot predict what will happen with our relationship.

I believe in fate, and I believe there is a perfect someone for everyone. I may have already met my ideal mate; then again, I may have not. I am leaving it for the stars in the sky to decide, and allow things to occur in their own good time. ▣

Photo by Jeff Antonucci

The Puzzle

by Emily Newick

I want to stay in my own house in Maine. Please, don't make me go to Florida," my grandmother Nanu argued from her bed. It was 7:30 in the morning; my father had just explained that they were going to leave for Florida where she lives in the winter. Dad reassured her that she loved the friendly people and warm weather.

While sitting in bed looking both defiant and nervous, Nanu effectively defended her position. If she stayed in Maine, she would be near her family; they wouldn't have to travel; her friend Sally could move in and live with her; if the weather was bad, she would just hole up. She was thoughtful and logical, presenting a formidable argument for staying. But, it was not possible.

Nanu has Alzheimer's, which has wiped away her short-term memory. She doesn't recall that she has spent the last six winters in Florida until she arrives and sees her friends. She reiterated, "I do not want to go to Florida. I do not know anyone there."

My dad patiently convinced her that he would go with her and that she would enjoy Florida. It is painful to listen to Nanu describe her desire to stay in Maine. It is her home. She has no memory of Florida, so naturally she is scared about going there. There is no easy method of convincing Nanu that she will be okay.

During a lull in the conversation, Nanu suddenly said, "What are we arguing about?"

My father smiled and said, "I was explaining that you need to get up so we can catch a plane to Florida."

Nanu replied, "Which side of the argument was I on?" Instantly recognizing the absurdity of her question, she leaned back in laughter. Humor in an awkward situation has become a frequent occurrence with Nanu: She will forget something and wind up laughing.

When I was young, my grandmother was active and energetic. Our biggest concern was keeping her in one place for more than thirty minutes. In the past five years her memory has progressively deteriorated. She cannot remember what you just told her, where she left her purse, or whom you just introduced to her. She has acquired new habits that mystify the family, including squirreling away things in the back of closets and under beds, or taking everything out of a kitchen cabinet and placing it on the counter. She becomes frustrated when she realizes her memory problem inhibits her. Simple daily occurrences such as losing her purse epitomize the metamorphosis that has occurred.

I, too, have been transformed from the child I was to the person I am now. I wear dresses without crying or arguing. I do not suck my thumb, and I travel without my blanket. Nanu and I have reversed roles. When I was young, Nanu was the "adult," the "authority," taking my sister and me to the beach, to the Goldenrod for ice cream, to feed the ducks and unfortunately, on occasion, to try on dresses. Nanu would present us with birthday presents that would excite us for weeks, like the space-suits she bought one year. But, now I take her on an afternoon drive or to lunch at the Goldenrod. In reality, now she is the child.

It is painful to watch her become incapacitated. She has lost her independence. Nanu can remember her past abilities, but cannot perform them. It is hard for her to realize that she must rely on others.

Although at times it seems like Nanu has lost every-thing because of Alzheimer's, I realize that she is still very much alive. It is easy to become depressed and remem-ber when life was easier for her. I need to be patient and forgiving. Nanu will ask me the same question five times during one meal, and each time I will honestly respond. It doesn't help to tell her, "I just told you that." After the question is repeated many times, it is tempting to become frustrated, but I cannot. I must remember what Nanu has taught me: a positive attitude, patience and an eagerness to unselfishly help others.

A mind afflicted with Alzheimer's is like an old puzzle. Over the years we have fit the pieces together to form a clear picture. Every detail is in its proper place; every piece fits. As time goes by, some of those pieces break. Later, pieces are lost, which makes the puzzle harder to keep together. Yet, the shapes are still there and we can see what the picture was. But, as more and more of the pieces are lost, the puzzle's picture becomes harder to decipher until, finally, the picture is gone. The rate the pieces disappear is a mystery. Sometimes lost pieces can be found for a while before they become lost again.

There is no way of knowing how long the picture will last—a week, a month, a year, many years.

Nanu's memory is a mystery to me. Although she is no longer the adult she once was, she continues to teach me. She still thinks logically and, like many with Alzheimer's, her long-term memory is a treasure. She has never given up. She displays a positive outlook with humor as her ally. Her fascination with education, technology and travel has been passed to each of her grandchildren. I hope that I can keep the puzzle for a long time. However, I know there will come a time when the puzzle will have too many missing pieces and the picture will fade. ◙

No Joy Ride

by Erik DeRosa Lattimore

You can't imagine how happy I was when my big one-six birthday finally arrived. I got my learner's permit the very next day after passing the easy but lengthy test that is a deterrent only for the completely driving illiterate. One of the questions was what to do when coming to a stop sign; how basic is that? And another asked which was the passing lane. There were a couple of hard questions, but not enough to postpone my rite of passage. After a couple of weeks, they mailed my permit, which displays the worst photo ever taken of me.

I would have liked to go out driving the day I got my permit, but my parents didn't prove as eager. I spent another week suggesting, "Hey, look, the weather is perfect for driving, and it's a great time for me to practice." I'm not sure what they were worried about, but I'm sure I'll find out when I have my own kids.

I'd had some experience driving, so I figured I was all set. Even my mother told me I was driving quite well for a first-timer. I was surprised to hear this because the whole time we were on the road, she yelled at me and made comments. After five minutes behind the wheel, I was wondering why I had been so eager to get myself into this; it wasn't going to be any joy ride.

I didn't consider myself a bad driver, but I did realize there was more to learn. My mother's analysis after three hours of driving time under my belt? I accelerated too fast, braked too quickly, stayed too far to the right and followed cars too closely. After five hours, she had narrowed the list down to driving too fast.

I thought, *Driving too fast?* How ironic that a person who was driving too fast would be the one to hold up traffic. No matter how slowly I went, my mom still told me to apply the brake. I would, and watch the line of cars in my rearview mirror grow longer and longer. I found my mother's tendency to hyperventilate as I drove unnecessary and somewhat distracting. Even on back roads, her heart rate was probably twice its normal. I concluded that the only place I could drive that would allow her any relaxation would be a deserted road in Arizona.

Not wanting to put her (or myself) through this same torture day in and day out, I tried to enlist some other help. Naturally, I turned to my father. Since he's the laid-back, easygoing type, I figured he'd be ideal. After more thought, I realized my error, recalling that he has a bad heart and short temper, which could be a lethal combination if I made a serious mistake. One day, my mother told me that my grandpa wanted to take me driving, and that he had suggested practicing at the cemetery because of its many twists and turns. The word cemetery reminded me of my older brother's little accident that totaled the car. I could only imagine going off the road there and taking out tombstones. Our family would probably never be allowed to be buried there.

Finally, God sent some good fortune my way: My older brother came home to attend a local college. He was the perfect candidate for the job; he couldn't yell at me for simple, honest mistakes, because I knew too well how he drove. How did he crash in the cemetery in the first place?

In the end, they all taught me to drive, and I'm glad. My mom would tell me what I was doing, constantly talking and pointing out the obvious. My dad, a little more serious, gave me a taste of how the instructor would act during my road test. It was nice driving with my brother to get experience. When it came down to it, the only way to improve was with hours of practice. It must be tough to teach a teenager anything since we all suffer from the chronic belief that we're always right and know everything. Everyone, watch out! Another one is on the road! 🔲

Photo by Ed Jaffe

Climbing Out
of the Cereal Bowl

by Julie Nicole Boucher

I t was the time in August when summer begins to get stale and nights cool just enough for us to welcome sheets again. The rhythm of crickets nestled along house foundations and flowerbeds starts to lose its charm with people rolling over restlessly, longing for some new song to usher them to sleep. Then it hit me . . . in a matter of weeks, summer would be closing its screened doors. Everywhere I looked, it seemed, there was something prodding gently and reminding me that it would all be ending soon.

"So, this is really it, huh?" Her usually fiery brown eyes searched my face, looking defeated, yet holding a sharp clarity from crying. "You know, you could always just live with us. Then, next year we could graduate together. We just can't *not* graduate together. . . . We can't." Her voice started to crack again on that last word.

I fought within myself to find some answer that would justify why suddenly everything in the world that just a second ago had been so concrete was sliding away, leaving us both alone. Streaking thoughts of a new town, like falling stars, with jobs, stability, a public high school with TVs in every classroom, all died before they fully formed and I opened my mouth.

Her left leg (the one with a life all its own when she's upset) moved spasmodically up and down in tight, anxious little motions. . . . God, if I ever accomplish my dream of someday becoming a journalist, the first time I hear artillery gunfire, I'm not going to jump, and I'm not gonna be frightened. I'll already be comfortable with the sound. . . . It'll be the tap, tap, tap, tap, tap, tap, tapping from the flat bottom of her tennis shoe against the slab of concrete we were sitting on. That single sound was probably responsible for blowing out insects' ears all over the neighborhood.

The mountains were all that was visible, rolling across the horizon as always, nothing changing their primitive agenda, offering no answers. But then, I didn't really expect them to. . . . Mount Greylock, the highest point in all of Massachusetts, raised itself a little, the blinking lights of the radio tower beaming proudly, mockingly, into the dark of the oncoming night. We both shivered as light became scarcer and scarcer and each blade of grass was encircled in cool spheres of dew. Huddling into the worn comfort of an old boyfriend's sweatshirt, quietly rocking back and forth, we watched the newly born night sky becoming a dark screen for the memories about to play.

Once, when I was really small, my mom had been sitting on the front step after weeding the garden, drinking orange Kool-Aid from an old jam jar, watching the sunset. I had run in from the yard and stared into her face for a long moment, waiting for her to acknowledge my presence. She gathered me in her arms, the hard bone of her chin resting on the top of my head with a comforting pressure. Pointing to each of the mountains around us, I asked, "Mom, what's over that one?" And patiently, she named every hill town in Berkshire County. Then she told a story I'd heard all my childhood—about how we lived at the very bottom of a big cereal bowl, and all the mountains that reached up to touch the sky were the sides of it. . . . I remember shifting deeper into the warmth of her arms, feeling secure and content with everything in place, everything complete.

Tonight, though, those mountains were not such compassionate friends. I almost laughed, but it stuck in my throat as a thought hit me: I used to ask so excitedly about what was over those mountains, but as I grew older, the security they assured bored me. In time, I'd grown to resent the familiarity and safety of my home. Now I was leaving, and in the face of the wave I wanted to shy away from those experiences and people that lay beyond.

It was both strange and ironic that something I'd always associated with protection in many ways basically choked us out. The mountains themselves stifled the area with lack of diversity, smothered with limited opportunities, and eventually, in the end, spat us out.

For a long time, dark circles had worn hollows below my father's eyes. Updated resumés and newspapers all found a new home on the kitchen table, and an anxious path worked itself into the floor in front of the telephone. Real truth in those black days confirmed all the times I'd heard, "You'll never make it unless you leave this area. There's no future here." It struck me how right they all were, and how much it hurt to find that simple truth to be correct. . . .

Now, as much as the gentle landscape beckoned, and the mountains unfolded their ancient, flowing arms, other forces, even more powerful than the pull of the land, were propelling us to different places . . . places where the former beauty paled, where seasons spin together so fast it was difficult to distinguish one from the next. For the first time I'd miss an autumn fast in coming, like an afghan hastily thrown over the mountains, crocheted in bold, contrasting colors . . . miss the stark winters and the black tree branches clashing against the stony mountains . . . miss that harsh kind of beauty.

I looked over at her, my best friend, my soul mate, my partner, the only person who really knew me. For the first time, the kaleidoscope shifted, and I saw her removed, independent of my friendship. A panic rose— what would I do without her? Then something sharp and gleaming tore inside and my eyes shed the evidence. We continued to sit there for a long while, connected in our separate silence and sadness.

The next morning, after the birds first heralded the new day and then hushed, the moving van came. It was a loud yellow Ryder, announcing that we were just about gone. And for the sake of the neighbors, cradling warm cups of early morning coffee, peeking out of kitchen windows, the scarlet lettering on its side verified any questions. Yeah, there were other places beyond the rim of those mountains, and knowing that provided some relief.

The heavy steel door rolled down with a bang and the snap of hurry-up-and-say-good-bye finality. One last time we walked through the house. Footsteps echoed on the floor, and the bare walls stood open and patient, quietly waiting for their next occupants. In the distance, the cereal bowl loomed, spilling over the salty sting of tears and memories of sugar-sweetened milk. ◙

Photo by Lea Ann Coreau

The Spigot

by Amybeth Gardner

She placed her slender, pale fingers around the handle, loosened its grip, and held a brown cup beneath it while the water flowed unevenly. The heat seemed to be engulfing her; the humidity, she finally concluded, was the reason she could hardly breathe.

"Stifling," she explained out loud. "Ridiculous." The girl blew her bangs off her forehead for a moment with her hot breath, as the cup continued to fill with the rusty-tinted water. *Thank God I'm not drinking this,* she thought. She was young, seventeen maybe, tall, thin and average-looking. She had a drawn-out look in her eyes, a look that told strangers she had been weathered, used even, older than she actually was. Peeling this layer off, her tan skin was evident, her long, dark-brown tresses pretty, even though she would never admit it. The girl waved her hands back and forth under the stream of water, as it would help cool her entire body; she tried to smile, but the more she tried, the more tears filled her eyes.

"Hard," she replied. "This is going to be hard."

Overhead crows flew, squawking at the heat as she wiped the beaded sweat from her nose; she dreamed of the air conditioners in the store she had just visited, the department store with the television sets and the radios. Gravestones were all around; she thought of the families who must mourn the loss of those who lay beneath the glassy black marbled rocks. She marveled at some of the flowers and held the cup of water close to her chest. She had only brought one rose, one single rose that she had asked the florist to wrap with baby's breath in cellophane. He had given her a peculiar look upon her request.

"But we just got in this wonderfully new pink and purple paper . . . purple would complement this rose in a lovely manner." The florist had tried to convince her, but the girl again requested the cellophane.

"The rose will be outside," she tried to explain without being blunt, "out in the sun, in the rain, on the ground."

The florist was utterly confused, so the girl just smiled as he continued to place the ferns and baby's breath around the rose.

The girl picked up her rose and the water, which now seemed even ruddier. She walked slowly to the grave without a stone; there were no markers, only old, decaying flowers, and a few new ones with even fewer planted firmly into the ground. She had tried to visit this grave so many times, but could not bring herself to do it, telling herself that the violent death of this person was hard enough and she didn't want to be like everyone else, making this a shrine where all her friend wanted was to be laid to rest.

Eventually, the girl felt guilty, and so she came. There she stood, breathing in the hot air and then expelling it, breathing hard, heavily, nervously, thinking maybe she should talk out loud, maybe she should water the flowers, leave the rose and go. She looked longingly at her car. She wanted to jump in and drive off. She breathed in once more, placed the rose at the head of the grave and kneeled, her hands clasped tightly, mouth chattering, face sweaty and tears running, flowing down her face. She wiped them away, her body shaking.

"I miss you," she said in a voice that was trying so hard not to sound weak. "I miss you so much, and everyone thinks I'm crazy because I miss you so. They tell me to move on, but I just can't sometimes."

Now her words were pouring out like an overflowing stream; she found great comfort in once again confiding in her friend.

"They don't understand me," she cried harder, "and they tell me I have no right to be acting like this. I never used to cry so much. . . . Now look at me! The only person who ever understood me is gone. . . . You were the only one."

She thought that perhaps her friend felt guilty now, so she gathered herself together and sat up tall. "You left me a lot of people to talk to: your sister, your friend Donna, your mother, the people you work with. But I'm just too busy comparing them all to you. I want to cry to you."

She didn't want to say anymore. She was tired, exhausted from the tears, taking sporadic breaths. She felt relieved to have let out the negative energy, the anger, pain and hurt. She didn't have to hide it anymore. She got up and brushed off her knees; they were imprinted with pebbles, grass and leaves from kneeling.

She thought maybe her eyes were red and her white shorts were dirty. She poured the water over the flowers, which they drank immediately; the geraniums, the pansies, and some exotic pink flower she had never seen before, with little blossoms and yellow centers.

The rose she left seemed insignificant; she felt like she owed her friend more, but had found nothing else in the florist's shop that suited her taste more than a single rose. The girl kneeled, said a brief prayer she made up and said good-bye to her teacher. ▣

Art by Erica Hillary Trestyn

Grandma

by Linda Liu

She told me many a tale
of China,
of her own mother
a concubine in a big house
rich with the smell of incense and
jasmine tea.
Her tiny feet would tread
softly upon the earth
wrapped in a myriad of swaddling binds
confining the dreams
the wishes
of a lifetime.
Yet she would smile
gazing upon their tininess
others praising their beauty.

Now she sits in her rocking chair
drinking Lipton orange pekoe
lips parched and silent.
I approach and ask
"Can I do anything for you, Grandma?"
She does not answer
then I see

the Miracle Ear lying on the dresser.
I tap her shoulder
whisper question in deaf ear,
she looks up at me
stroking my face with those thin hands
blue veins encased in thin layer of flesh
yellow as parchment,
old as the years passed away.
Smiling she answers,
"You be good girl."

I take her hands in mine:
Grandma, I want to see you fly
and be free and laugh high
show fierce sparkle in your eye,
waltz wildly through the night
let nothing pass you by.
What can I do but
walk slowly away
watching her rock
take off tiny slippers
to rub painful feet?

Hot Lips

by Lauren Sue Asperschlager

He calls me Hot Lips. Through the thick glasses encircling his weary eyes, I see a sparkle when he says it. His own lips pull back slowly, revealing coffee-stained teeth as he laughs. I've heard it before, but still I laugh. Not at his wispy white hair much like a maniacal scientist in a laboratory. Not at bizarre expressions like "Hot dog!" that unconsciously escape from his mouth. Not at the makeshift plunger mute he cups over the end of his trombone during jazz solos, or even at the fact that he dares to play jazz in church. A rebel. My laughter mingles with that of a seventy-three-year-old rebel, but it didn't always.

A cold metal folding chair greeted me that day long ago when I entered the room. I avoid it. Glancing at the unfamiliar scene, I stand, afraid to touch anything for fear it will crumble. Yellowed snapshots watch me, scrutinizing the amateur. "Ah, another victim," they whisper. Ashamed to be intimidated by frozen black and white faces, I direct my eyes toward the opposite wall. I break the tension by laughing at a sign partially hidden behind the mountain of musical paraphernalia. "Never Teach a Pig to Sing . . ." Who is this guy?

"It wastes your time and annoys the pig," a voice from

behind me finishes. Startled, I gasp. Not a quick gasp that can be covered to avoid embarrassment. No, this was one of those high-pitched squeals I was eager to reach out and grab the moment it exited my mouth. Reluctantly, I peer at the man standing behind me.

A caramel-colored corduroy jacket with elbow patches just barely conceals an ink stain on his blue denim shirt. I glance at his faded jeans. Probably hasn't bought a new pair in years. Worn, soiled Nikes complete the ensemble. Yet, a sense of order and dignity polishes his appearance, mends the frayed edges.

"Sit down," he says directly, the smile sliding off his face, replaced by intense concentration. I sit. A red book appears on a black metal stand. Rummaging through the pile, he pulls out a case, not as dusty as the others. The handle isn't even broken. Maybe there is hope. From it emerges polished brass, oiled valves, greased slides. He places the object in my hands, which receive it tentatively. He opens the red book. Except for the sentence "When you see six sharps, what key signature are you in?" and the inescapable phrase "Practice, practice, practice," I remember nothing else about that day.

Now, months later, it is Sunday morning, and the congregation is before me, and the rebel behind me in Sunday best. He traded his Nikes for black polished leather. I adjust the stand, placing the music on the right side as always. "That way your bell can face straight out, kid. Never forget it." I hadn't. Taking a deep breath, I place my cornet on my lips. Sensing I am finally prepared, he raises the baton, chipped plastic with a worn wooden handle. Out of the corner of my eye, I see his arm move, the baton coming down slowly. The first note echoes in the chapel simultaneously.

I cringe at the sound, hearing a swift gasp from the observers. "Just keep going, kid." I do. With the rebel behind, his baton conducting each note, right or wrong, I continue. The melody soars higher, my confidence growing. Imagining the intensity on his face, I relax my tense muscles. Sensing his arthritic hand shaking with each sweeping motion, I cease my own nervous trembling. As his asthma leaves him short of breath and coughing in the background, I fill my lungs and release the oxygen into the warm brass against my lips. We reach the last note together, my face numb, my lips contorted to reach the upper limits of the musical realm. I hold the note, waiting for his cut-off. When it finally ends, there is no applause. But behind me, through a smile of coffee-stained teeth, four words emerge that only I can hear: "Good job, Hot Lips." ▣

Thank You

by Raabia Shafi

My mother was running back and forth through the kitchen trying to beat the clock and be ready before the guests came. As usual, my grandparents were first to arrive, right on time. They took their customary seats: my grandfather on the armchair facing my grandmother, who took the end of our three-person leather couch, always inviting us to sit next to her for a warm hug. The glittery black suit she wore was beautiful silk, giving her an almost majestic glow.

"Do you need my help, Lubna?" my grandmother—my Apa Ji—called to my mom in the kitchen.

"Yes, Apa," she said. "Please get my stubborn daughter in the shower and dressed before the guests arrive!"

I was only six years old, but I can still remember how my mother had been asking me for two hours to get ready. It was not the shower that made me put it off; it was the lavender shalwaar kameez with silver zigzags I would have to wear that made me procrastinate. That Pakistani suit was so itchy!

When my grandmother found me hiding in the basement, she took a firm hold of my arm, although her grasp was gentle.

"Let's go, Raabia. Come on . . . the guests will be here any minute."

With a grouchy look, I crawled from beneath a table and followed her to the bathroom.

"You know," she began, rinsing the soapsuds off my shoulders, "you need to start learning how to cooperate with your family. Your mom has been cooking and cleaning since morning, and all she asked of you was to be ready before the guests come. You really ought to stop being so stubborn and start helping your family out."

She dried my skin with the towel with such familiarity you could tell she'd done this many times for her five children. Then Apa Ji pulled the dreaded purple suit over my head, combed my hair and had me ready in four minutes.

"Thank you, Apa Ji," I grumbled, strictly out of respect, of course.

"You're most welcome. You are looking very smart," Apa Ji replied with a smile of motherly satisfaction.

After the party, I ran upstairs to my pink-wallpapered bedroom and changed into my cotton pajamas. The suit had irritated me all evening.

* * *

Recently, my grandmother was diagnosed with cancer. Returning home from the hospital, Apa Ji was weak from chemotherapy and needed assistance with almost everything. I stayed with my grandparents for the weekend, helping whenever I could.

With my head resting on Apa Ji's lap, I flipped through a catalog and helped her pick out a wig. I opened all the curtains to let in the warm sunlight that had been hiding in the shadows during the long weeks she had been in the hospital.

I was in the kitchen unloading the dishwasher when Apa Ji called me to help her in the shower. She grabbed my arm for support with the same gentleness she'd used to drag me into the shower eleven years earlier. I squeezed the loofah sponge over her feeble shoulders, then gently patted the towel over her and helped her out. I dressed her in the loose shalwaar kameez she had left on the towel rack. She looked at my face with sad eyes and asked me to comb what was left of her thinning hair.

"Thank you for all of your help, Raabia," she said when I finished.

"You're most welcome," I replied with a melancholy smile.

Of all the people I have had the honor of knowing and, better yet, being related to, Apa Ji with her determination to live her life has taught me the most about human integrity. Faced with what has been the most intense challenge presented to my family, Apa Ji's courageous spirit is the reason we are learning to cope.

"Your grandmother is an extremely strong-willed person," people used to say after telling me long stories about the work she had done to support her family, who immigrated to London in the '60s. Without fully understanding, I always nodded and went on with my own work. Now, when people tell me of Apa Ji's strong will, I smile with sincere pride because I have witnessed firsthand her energetic devotion to her family and life. Apa Ji taught me not to pity others but to empathize with their needs and help in a way that does not violate their dignity. I have learned a great deal from my grandmother merely by observing the strength of her smile. She will always be my hero. ▣

Photo by Pamela J. Torok

The Stillness of a Picture

Fiction by Esther Ling

The sailboat looked as if it were going to sail off the edge of the world. Faintly etched against the horizon, its billowing white sails were barely visible against the cloudy gray sky. *That's what I want to do,* I thought as I watched from my vantage point on the rocks. *I want to fall off the edge of this world so no one will ever find me.* With the sound of water in my ears, I let my mind sing in time with the wind. I become a part of nature.

I know my mother is up on land, watching me and wringing her hands. She doesn't know whether or not to tell me to come up from the rocks. She doesn't know how to comfort me. I imagine nothing quite like this has ever happened to her. Perhaps she is contemplating whether to come down, hug me and whisper comforting words. But she knows better. She knows it will only drive me even farther away than I already am.

This rock beneath me is hard. It's a good thing I remembered a blanket. As I watch, the waves grow. Some rocks visible only one hour ago are completely submerged. This day suits my mood. Perhaps most people prefer the sun, but not me. You know the line, "Every cloud has a silver lining"? Well, all my life I've searched for that silver lining. It doesn't exist. It's just one of the world's ploys to try to keep people interested in life.

"Chelsea! Please come up from there! The tide is getting higher." I knew my mother would give in to the urge to call me. But I do not answer. She's only doing what she thinks a good mother would do. She doesn't know who I am. She, the woman who walked out of my life when I was seven years old to live with another man, is the last person who would ever understand me.

She left a note the day she left. Something about how I wasn't supposed to blame her for leaving, that the whole situation was my father's fault. Perhaps it was. I don't remember exactly what that letter said; I showed it to Dad and he tore it up in rage. "Never believe what that witch says to you," he said as he became the human paper shredder. I never believed her. I don't recall them fighting much. I suppose they were smart enough to fight when I wasn't around or was asleep. Perhaps, my mind is just subconsciously blocking it out. Either way, I don't remember much of life with my mother.

I remember little things—how she complained about the pictures of the ocean my father kept around the house. She used to say, "Steven, darling, those pictures—they irritate me. I almost feel like I'm drowning with every step I take." Then, of course, Dad would retort with some comment how she didn't appreciate real art. I don't remember her ever really hugging me or telling me that she loved me. She spent a lot of time out of the house. Where she went, I'm not quite sure. I only knew that instead of having my mother call me in for dinner like other kids, I was given a watch so I would know what time to come in.

I remember her wearing the most colorful clothing she could find. Against the drab decor of our house, she hurt my eyes as if she were the sun. She would play music, full of light and major harmonies, while my father retreated into his study filled with broken chords and melodies. Her moods would change like the weather. One moment, she would be more vivid than the brightest star; the next, even the cloudiest day wouldn't hold a candle to her. She had whitish-blonde hair that was almost always loose and free to play in the wind. Oh, and her eyes! They are practically the only trait I got from her: emerald green, they sparkled like emeralds themselves.

My mother was a chameleon. When she was in the house, she was quiet and her steps cautious. But once she stepped outside into the world, the chains fell and her most brilliant colors appeared. Strings of words would stream endlessly from her. Gone was all the prudence, all the wariness. Her step was lighter and her laughter bounced over every plane. She was a kaleidoscope. No matter which way the world turned or twisted, she came up with a new way to look beautiful and be happy.

I know she doesn't really care about me. She doesn't know how to comfort me. She doesn't know what it's like to lose the most important person in your life. I do. My father abandoned me in a way no one ever could have expected. He died suddenly one night. The priest told me that an angel came and beckoned his spirit and he couldn't resist, not even for me. I know my mother isn't actually worried about me. She is just worried about what the neighbors will think if anything happens to me. They already know that she left me and Dad. Now, with this new turn of events, she wants to prove to herself and everyone else that she can be a good mother. She wasn't there for all the moments I was growing up, and I'm not about to let her charge into my life now. Not that there's much to see anyway. Now, there is only . . . emptiness.

My father used to collect pictures of the ocean. Framed in wood, gilded with gold, they had resting places all around the house. Sometimes, they would depict a raging storm and sometimes the calm within the eye of a hurricane. "In pictures, beauty never fades," he always used to say. Often, he would lock himself in the study and just stare at the pictures. When he died, my mother insisted on selling all of them. She said that they reminded her of him and whenever she saw them, they made her cry. She lied. Now, all I have to remind me of him is the ocean itself.

My father was a photographer. He saw most of the world through pictures and a camera's viewfinder, not taking time to come up for a fresh look at his whole surroundings. The world passed him by as he turned slowly with his camera. He was a loner. My mother was the only person he ever dated. After she left, he regressed to isolation. I was his only company.

I've always been a loner. The pale girl with the thin, long brown hair. When all the other girls started going out with the guys who had been friends since childhood, going to dances and parties and wearing makeup, I stayed home, sat with my father, looking at the pictures. When I was little, my dad didn't know how to take care of a little girl. My hair was never cut; it just grew long and straight. I was always dressed as a little boy. Maybe that's part of why I am the way I am.

I miss my father. I miss his reassuring presence whenever anything went wrong. I miss the times that we would just sit together, silently, and look at the beautiful pictures of the ocean. I miss the times he used to teach me how to take pictures, arrange flowers Japanese style and examine gems for their true value. Now, the imprint of his face is already fading in my mind.

As I watch the water, I can see light reflected and refracted off the waves at different angles. The ocean is ever changing. Now that I think of it, the real beauty in the ocean is its never being the same from one second to another, unlike the stillness of the pictures in my head. I wish I could become a part of the waves and just flow wherever the current carried me. But as I watch, I know that it's not possible. Carefully, I maneuver around the rocks and head back toward land. ▣

First Kiss

by Nicole Flannery

TV blaring on,
we sit on the couch,
bodies stiff,
Nervous.
Oblivious to the voices
"Oh, John, I love you so!"
It spoke, a soap opera.
His hand grasped mine,
the other a remote.
Click, said the TV
Hello, said his eyes,
as they penetrated mine
pupils dilated
Man, I like him so much,
Whoosh, heat rushed to my face,
Bright red, ears warm.
Smile,
God, I'm hot. (hands caress my cheekbones)
He smiles
Eyes close, waiting, waiting
come on, I can't take it.
Lips touch
Softly.
First Kiss.

Roots and Branches

by Julie White

The sun playfully flickered and danced among the rich green leaves swaying gracefully in the soft summer breeze. Slowly, I rubbed my hand over the rough bark of the tree trunk, feeling each groove and bump, and remembering. As I pressed harder, the surface caused my hand to burn and ache, the same feeling that engulfed my heart as I sat there pressing, remembering. This had been our tree; it belonged to the six of us, better known as the "six pack." When we were little we spent hours playing in the branches of the enormous oak tree that sat defiantly in Chelsea's front yard.

After meeting in first grade, Courtney, Nichole, Chelsea, Maggie, Sarah and I took it upon ourselves to establish our pact of friendship. It started by sharing Crayola magic markers, then progressed to after-school play days, elementary-school crushes, swapping snacks and bonding over games at recess. Whether we were involved in sports, Girl Scouts, dance lessons or summer days at the beach, we were together; it was the only way to be.

For a moment I paused, the echo of childish giggles and jibber-jabber rang in my ears. I felt the pain again as

I gazed at the tree's outstretched arms that seemed so full of memories. The aching crept from my hand to my stomach. The tire swing was empty, hanging from the tattered rope, worn from years of tugging and swinging. I watched it swinging silently on what seemed to be the last strands of rope, nowhere to spin but in circles with the wind. I wondered when the rope began to fray and tear, as if it were aware of its deterioration. Over and over I traced the grooves of the trunk with my fingers, searching for memories.

I traveled back. Suddenly, we were in middle school. Crushes became more serious; we were interested in hair spray, music, shopping for matching outfits; everything was done as a whole. School dances were the most important social events; no one could miss even one. Our plans for the future changed weekly, but no matter what, we promised to be together. "Never forget the six pack."

Before we were ready, off we went to high school. The reaction upperclassmen gave us came as a shock; they actually thought we would someday grow apart. But ideas like that were ludicrous. We had a pact that no one could break (except maybe one of us). When the whole group turned out not to be interested in soccer, it seemed even crazier—we were supposed to act as one! But that was part of growing up. We learned that each of us was different and liked different things. Sometimes this reality hurt, as growing often does.

I breathed in deeply, inhaling the scent of the tree, continuing to rub the grooves and even its weather wounds and scars. I wondered if the tree was hurt by them, if it still felt the pain caused years before. I thought of the summer the first real fight occurred and how the words, spat out unintentionally, still stung each of us inside. How we tried to cover the anger with smiles, but underneath were scarred. The branches seemed to sprout from the trunk wildly. I found it ironic how they diverted from the same origin, yet were so different.

My eyes blurred over, the tree became fuzzy as hot tears streamed down my cheeks and fell onto our tree. I ached for our innocent days filled with giggling and carefree attitudes. What did it take to erase the words, the actions, we had never planned in any of our futures? Burning spread throughout my hand that traced the grooves, while inside me the burning continued as I traced my memories.

My tears ceased as I studied the tree and began to discover an almost relieving realization. Like the branches of our tree, we may have grown in different directions, but our roots would remain as one. Our lives will always be a special part of the others'. Sometimes it hurts to realize that we have moved on from our past, but the past only makes us stronger and ready to welcome the best that is yet to come. 回

7 Everyday Happenings

Photo by Yaniris Mejia

Italian Voice

by Lisa Schottenfeld

V orrei spiegarvie, Dio! Qual é l'affanno mio . . ." My squat, shrewd-looking voice teacher switched off the record and turned to examine me with the gleam in her eye I'd quickly learned to dread.

"Whaddya think?" she asked expectantly, settling back into the slight groove she'd worn in her piano bench.

I swallowed nervously, desperately searching for a response. Open-minded, I scolded the devil perched on my shoulder. *You've got to be open-minded!* "It was . . . um . . . interesting," I managed.

She grinned wildly. "Well, that's what you're gonna sound like by the time I'm through with ya!" she declared triumphantly. "Whaddya think about that?"

I sensed my afternoon snack planning a swift return trip up my esophagus. "Wha—what do you mean? We couldn't go any lower down the scale than that? I—I really don't think I can pull that off," I stammered helplessly.

"You'll see," she trilled on a high E. I couldn't help but shiver.

Within weeks, I had received my first aria, *"O cessate de piagarmi."* The name certainly sounded pretty. "What does it mean?" I asked excitedly, anticipating wild tales of true love and frolicking under the stars. Maybe this opera thing wouldn't be so bad after all.

"Oh . . ." she responded tiredly, "it's about a guy who's sick of the world and trying to figure out how to commit suicide. Why don't you start at measure eight?"

I left that teacher a month later with a dire hate of anything operatic. I was welcomed back with open arms to Opera Haters Anonymous, the exclusive association founded by my father and younger sister. The only membership requirement was that all participants had to clamp their hands over their ears and grimace, as if undergoing an amputation without anesthesia, any time strains of *Carmen* or *Madame Butterfly* floated over the dinner-table conversation as a result of my mother's efforts to win us over to the "beauty" of opera. All I knew was that it wasn't going to happen—no Italian suicides for me, thank you very much.

Several months later, however, I found myself back in a cramped practice room with a new voice teacher. I'd had my mother thoroughly grill this one before signing me up to ensure that she was, in fact, a musical-theater instructor and not some aria freak.

Paula seemed amiable enough. In fact, she completely understood my severe case of I-hate-to-sing-anything-above-a-high-C phobia, and I decided we were teacher-pupil soul mates. She began ticking off her most-loved composers and performers to see if we could find any in common: "Stephen Sondheim, Carole King, Kathleen Battle . . ."

"Kathleen Battle?" I asked curiously. I wondered if she was some sort of folk singer.

Paula's eyes lit up at the mere repetition of the name. "You've never heard Kathleen Battle sing? Oh, jeez—you've got to hear her! She has the most amazing voice in the world!" Duly excited, I promised to track down one of her recordings.

Curiously enough, I caught the name emblazoned on the side of a CD cover in my mother's vast collection of classical music. I pulled it out, thoroughly expecting it had been misplaced among the other albums labeled with unpronounceable names like Rossini's *Péchés de vieillesse* and Mozart's *Kammermusik mit Klarinette*. But my first glance at the CD cover made my heart sink. "Kathleen Battle Sings Mozart," it proclaimed proudly, showcasing a portrait of a heavily made-up woman in some sort of hideously frilled black dress.

Paula had failed me miserably.

I stuffed the CD back in its place, clearing it from my memory. Besides, if anyone had caught me glancing at such a recording, I could have lost my Opera Haters Anonymous membership.

Thankfully, Paula forgot about my supposed search for Kathleen Battle—at least for a few months. When she finally remembered and asked if I'd listened to any recordings, I lied through my teeth, saying I'd been unable to locate any. Paula raised her eyebrows and sighed. "All right," she said, "but you don't know what you're missing."

Feeling sufficiently guilty, I pulled the album off the shelf when I returned home. I'd give it two minutes of airplay, and then be through with opera forever. I pressed play with a grimace, fully expecting the room to overflow with the pretentious vibrato of yet another irritating soprano.

Instead, the violins began softly and were soon joined by the gentle chords of a piano. Before long, I realized a voice had slipped unobtrusively into the orchestra. The voice was far from pretentious. In fact, its clarity was improved only by its smooth, silvery tone. The foreign words, which sounded so cumbersome in the mouths of others, seemed to slide naturally off the singer's tongue.

I closed my eyes and slowly turned up the volume until the voice had wound itself into every corner of my mind, crowding out any unpleasant thoughts with its clear, bell-like quality. For several minutes I found myself in a state of near-meditation, enraptured by the soprano's quiet elegance. Before I knew it, I'd listened to nearly an hour of—gasp—Mozart's arias.

Paula knew what I'd been doing the instant she heard my voice on the phone. "So?" she asked hopefully.

"Can you teach me to sing like that?"

Paula laughed. 回

Playing the Game

by Noah Gordon

His hands danced. They danced with such agility and swiftness that they floated. The dark amber danced in time with the click of the clock—the rhythmic tick, like some odd metronome—and the hands tangoed and traversed the board. They played the game. It was the cracked and aged hands that attacked. They shot out, grabbing at a weakness and exploiting it, making you feel the power of the mind. The hand and mind were together, almost one. The hands, the dark amber hands, they would strike you down. They would dance. And they played the game.

The Square was like most of Manhattan. It was dirty, crowded and had a peculiar smell, like some putrid aura. Washington Square had seen worse times, though. The walkways used to be lined with crack vials, drug dealers with macho vendettas played out, and begging hobos and rampant whores crowding the entrances. Now that Giuliani was here, things were different. The threat of cameras, policemen and wide-eyed tourists was enough to keep away most of the crime. But ever since Bobby Fischer, Washington Square Park has been known for the game, the personalities and the masters who play.

I had always felt intimidated about playing in the Park.

It seemed to be something that was above me. But, actually, anyone could play there. I saw little kids, burned-out hobos and a retarded man sit down and challenge Dwight and the others. Anyone who had two dollars was invited to play; it didn't matter who you were, or weren't. I felt like I was degrading the game by playing there, taking it to a new low. You have to understand the atmosphere. It wasn't like those chess stores with nice tables and Mozart playing in the background. It was real. It was life. People were always yelling, smoking cigars or dope, sending pieces flying.

Dwight was beyond it, though. He was the one in the corner smiling and chatting with his opponent. I gravitated toward that corner, awed by the furious slapping of the clock and the laughter. I sat down and gawked at my opponent, Dwight. I gaped, stared, took in his presence, and wanted to run. His nimble hands flashed around the table and set the board. He gave me the white pieces, the advantage. As we played the first game it was like a courting game; we were introducing ourselves to each other. My pawn first shyly took position.

With a bold strike he met my pawn. My knight leaped and landed, fell over as I reached for the clock and I could feel my cheeks burn. He was cool and collected, and his bishop flew to the opposite side. I looked ravenously for a move, something to impress him and the tourist who stood behind me. I moved a pawn and waited for his next move. Queen out; he eyed me and smiled. I eyed the board and attacked with the bishop. Queen took pawn. Checkmate. I was stunned. I didn't feel it hit me until he chuckled and reached out his hand to shake mine. It was over. Scholar's mate, the most degrading of all. I sat in front of this man and smiled meekly.

He told me it was fine, and I looked up. The shame of my defeat slowly lifted and I set the pieces. I reached in my pocket for another few dollars and handed him two wrinkled bills. I was ready. We played together all that day, but the second game was mine. I felt the stare of the tourists on my back as I recuperated from my previous defeat. His hands danced the board and punished me with each move. But I answered, no longer dreading the consequences. He wore such a smile as he hit the clock. "You better get and go, boy. I'm not giving you a game."

Before I could think, it was out of my mouth: "You better get your knight out of my backyard."

I flinched, not even hearing myself but more echoing the cries I had heard from other players. He didn't look up, and I thought about how ridiculous I must have sounded. A white suburban kid talking like a punk off the street.

"Yeah, well, I suggest you get out of my way, because I'm here to do some business."

We laughed and the tourists commented that it was just like the movies. We talked trash and laughed like school buddies, friends from long ago, and the other people around just made me smile. Catcalls from all around the park rang out, and Dwight's followers, who were gathered around his table, made jokes and called each other names.

"Best move that bishop before someone gets hurt."

"That boy got some intentions on you, my man."

"Oh yeah, and I got an insurance policy on that, right here."

With a final sweep of his hands, he took my pawn. He slapped my king with the back of his hand, sending it off the board. Checkmate. But this time I was refreshed and overjoyed. I had another two dollars and a good friend to play the game with. I lost. I lost the game.

But the Park still chattered and reeked of dope. Tourists still flashed cameras and gobs of money. But now, I felt like one of the players. I knew the game and appreciated it. I wasn't there just to gawk. The tourists were like the pigeons, the sky rats, the gutter birds. They had no right to crowd this graceful and humble genius. They didn't deserve his presence.

Dwight was always nice to me. He took me under his wing and showed me the true meaning of the game. I've been back to see him and I'm now a part of the game there. My wins and losses in the Park are common lore with Dwight, since we are now good friends. As I look back on that first time, the courting period, I think of his hands. Those nimble, amber hands were my teachers and my tormentors, but never my opponent. 回

AUTHOR'S NOTE: *Dwight is not a fictional character. His characteristics have been blended with those of Sir Ed and Rich, all fabulous chess players. This story is basically the retelling of my first experience with the Park. Dwight does not talk trash much like the rest of the players, but is more like a gentleman. Sir Ed (a.k.a. Sir Ed the Tormentor, Sir Edward the First, or Eddy) has been in many chess movies, notably* Searching for Bobby Fischer. *Rich is one of the smartest men I know and has been known to quote Shakespeare, Thoreau and Hemingway.*

Photo by Jesse Legon

Fried Fish

by Joanna Sng

The sharp crackle of garlic hitting hot oil penetrated my sleep-induced grogginess. Stretching lazily, I peered over the arm of the couch where I had dozed. She was at it again. I still could not understand why she insisted on preparing lunch when there was someone to do such things.

My grandmother waddled out of the kitchen, wiping her hands on the corner of her grease-splattered apron as she clucked over the dirty dishes I had left scattered in the living room. She crossed the room to the couch and started fluffing the pillows beneath my head. I listened as she told me, for what seemed like the thousandth time, that no one could ever cook the way she does. Adamantly, she declared that I would find someone else cooking in her kitchen over her dead body. With another thump to the cushions, she rose from the couch and returned to the kitchen. I trailed after her, hoping to persuade her to leave its steamy heat. Without a glance toward me, she plopped two fish into the sputtering oil and garlic mixture. The frying fish turned a deep golden brown as I gazed into their sightless eyes.

My father would be coming downstairs soon and would demand to know why I had not offered to cook.

I looked again at the dented wok where the fish sizzled. Maybe I should cut vegetables or something. I picked up the dense metal chopper and began slicing the choy sum. As I moved the knife up and down over the leafy green vegetable, she put her wizened hand over mine, guiding my movements. In moments, the large leaves were reduced to a pile of spoon-sized pieces. She stepped back as I slid the vegetables off the chopping board into the pot of boiling water. I turned around to find her removing her apron. I stood stiffly as she slipped the worn linen over my head and tied the strings at the small of my back. She handed me her pair of wooden chopsticks and plodded out of the kitchen.

I retrieved the cooked fish from the wok and placed them on a bowl of rice. Stepping into the dining room, I found my grandmother sitting by the window, staring at the banana tree that grew just outside. A half smile played at the corners of her mouth. I sat beside her. She placed her arm around my shoulders and drew me to her side. I knew then that she had been waiting for me. Her joy was in giving me the chance to discover my own way. ▣

My Father's World

by David J. Stryker

I have grown up in a family whose love for music is unending. My growth has been marked not by when I started kindergarten or high school, but by musical standards. My father loved his music. On Saturday mornings he would lock himself in his office, pick up a copy of the *Times* and listen to music. He filled my mind with music which, when I was young, I resented. I never understood why he kept forcing me to listen to music and each time he did, I would always say, "Ugh, classical music again."

I did not know what to expect when I was invited to Tanglewood four years after his death. Would this remind me of those feelings of resentment, or bring me closer to him? I prepared like a young child getting ready for his first day of school. I put on a new white shirt and freshly ironed pants so I could fit in with the crowd. Approaching the "great lawn," as I later called it, I was awed by its beauty. I felt as if I had broken free of the bondage of everyday life. There was a slight breeze adding to an already perfect evening. The wispy clouds in the western sky were outlined in a warm crimson from the setting sun.

Children were scattered, playing games only they

could understand. Although the only people I knew were the friends I came with, I knew everyone that evening. This home was not mine, though; it was my father's. My father had been here often and told me his great memories. I was skeptical of how great a place could be when all you did was sit and listen to classical music. I soon realized, though, that my father's world was just waiting to be discovered.

Andre Previn walked onstage that night and looked up at the sky as if for divine guidance. The crowd erupted in cheers. Then suddenly no one dared even to whisper. The silence was eerie and with it came a sense of anticipation for what lay ahead. Previn picked up his baton and took command of his army of musicians.

The first chord of Beethoven's *Ninth Symphony* penetrated the crowd like a knife through flesh. It was not Beethoven's perfect combination of harmony and melody that changed me, but the fusion of the two to make a beautiful piece of music. For the first time I had a glimpse into my father's world and realized I had always had a piece of him inside me. Each note added another color to the cascading waterfall, and soon every color I could dream of was in the music. The final chord, though, brought all the colors together into a beautiful combination. It led each of us into an expansive open field of grass that seemed to go on forever. It took us by the hand and brought us to our idea of heaven.

It was my father's world I began to experience and enjoy, for this was now my heaven. My father never explained how to enjoy music. He simply exposed me to it, and even though I resented it, I now know why he made me listen. Every day I miss him, but music has brought us closer. When I heard that final chord, it concluded my journey, but in a sense it has just begun. I realize what he was trying to teach me, and there is so much I need to learn. I know each step will bring me closer to him. ◙

Photo by Adam Janko

Elizabeth

by Katherine Cincotta

*All is quiet on the car
ride home along back roads.
Outside the air is relaxed: sixty-eight degrees,
damp.*

*Small pearls of water
slide down the windows.*

*I stare through the
glass, follow black windshield wipers,
listen for the splash of puddles and
passing cars.*

*There is no music,
no conversation.
I don't notice.*

*There is no heavy air of awkwardness,
when it feels like time is stagnant.
No need to turn on the
radio or our voices.*

We are comfortable allowing ourselves
to be lost in the silence, in the mood, to listen only to
passing cars and rain.

I notice amidst
the breeze, and solitude,
that her breathing has become rhythmic, her
sapphire eyes have fallen, and she sleeps
as the lost pearls paint
the glass near her face.

Poster Boy

by Dan Durbin

Our changing aspects can be frightening since we like to think we know who we are. Usually it takes something drastic—a car accident or the loss of a loved one—to change. Most would not consider my "accident" drastic at all. It was something that I, along with just about everyone, do every day—I had a conversation, a simple, one-on-one conversation. But it changed my life.

We were at a leadership school. He looked like your typical Abercrombie and Fitch poster boy. Wearing jeans five sizes too big and a shirt five sizes too small, this preppy jock was so high on himself that he thought he could walk on water. Six times a day he called himself a "preppy jock," in case you forgot. He was everything society wanted him to be; he played his role well.

He was a heartthrob, or so I was told by many of the girls. He hung around me, probably because I was friends with the most attractive girl. By the end, I disliked him even more than before.

Tension grew between us, and people could tell I was irritated. Actually, I was jealous, and I knew it. Questions started hitting me, one after another: Why does he agitate me so much? Why don't I just talk to him? Am I really so insecure?

On one of the last nights of the program, I was talking to my attractive friend when he came in. People left, and I realized it was just us. We started saying things like, "Wow, the week has flown." I wanted him to leave, but he obviously didn't get my hints. He was pushing my patience. I thought, *What am I waiting for? Nobody else is here, and he needs someone to knock him off his cloud.*

"You know she doesn't want a relationship right now, right?" I asked.

"Yeah, I know," he muttered.

"Then why do you make it hard for her? Why don't you just accept the fact that you can't have this one right now?" I fired, hoping not to get a response.

"I've never met anyone like her. She's real. She isn't like those other girls who cake their faces with makeup and think it makes them beautiful. She's different," he replied.

"I know, she's great. But she doesn't need a relationship, especially long distance. You've been pushing my buttons being so persistent in pushing her. I don't trust you, especially with her," I commented.

"I want something different. I don't want to keep living like this," he said as he fought back the tears forming in his blue eyes.

"What do you mean?" I asked, a lump building in my throat.

"I can't stand being everyone's puppet! I've become what everyone wants me to be, instead of what I want to be," he said, releasing many years of bottled-up emotions.

This was the first time I saw him as he really was.

Many times that week he'd admitted being egotistical, yet he did nothing about it. He denied everything about himself that wasn't "cool." Even things he enjoyed, like playing the violin, were tossed aside at the thought—and fear—of rejection. He'd become a walking, breathing poster boy with no ambitions, thoughts or feelings of his own. He was the biggest case of insecurity I'd ever seen. He was a year younger than I was, and suddenly reminded me of someone—myself. My annoyance turned to compassion. I knew where he was coming from; it was like talking to a shadow. I'd had the willpower to change; he didn't. He needed encouragement from someone who had gone through it.

I'm not a saint. I'm not completely satisfied with myself, but I doubt many people are. Society expects perfection, or so we think. I thought all were in their utopia except me. I found out that real people have problems, and I've also felt empathy for those struggling with problems they choose not to show. Thus, now I am slower to judge. Fate only takes you so far, and then it's really up to you. If that guy hadn't taken an interest in my friend, I may never have talked to him and he would have continued in this same direction, which would have led him only to more frustration and anger. I don't know if he has made any permanent changes, but I know I tried to help. ▣

Signing

by Ilana Silverman

As the sun slowly peers from behind the maple trees, the butterflies in my stomach begin to dance. At first it is a slow, formal waltz, but by the time I enter the school bus, the pace turns to a lively swing. Those butterflies sure know how to jump, jive and wail. It is 7:00 A.M. You would think butterflies need their beauty sleep, but you'd be wrong.

It's not as if I am not prepared for the day. I am a second-year Sign Language student and do well in it. I even sign interpreted the Beatles' song "In My Life" at graduation last year. Yet visiting a school for the Deaf is still somewhat frightening. I haven't had much exposure signing with people who are actually Deaf. What if I can't remember how to sign something? Will I understand their signing? Will they laugh at me? Thoughts run rampant as the butterflies continue to boogie in my stomach.

Later, sitting in their cafeteria, I wait for my "buddy" to find me. We had been assigned students to escort us throughout the day. The room has suddenly become chaotic with students scrambling to find their partners. A girl wearing a green sweater, similar to the one I often borrow from my best friend, approaches me. She is holding a nametag that reads "Ilana."

"You?" She points at me, asking if this is my name.

I feel my fist naturally rise and shake. "Yes," I sign back. "My name is Ilana."

"My name is Jessica. Nice to meet you."

"Nice to meet you," I reply. I cannot believe this. Suddenly, everything we have learned comes together. I am actually communicating with a Deaf girl in Sign Language.

"How old are you?"

"What grade are you in?"

After we get past our greetings, we share a nervous laugh. We sit there, facing each other, wide smiles on our faces. Yet, we struggle to think about a topic—a substantial topic—to discuss. To keep the conversation going, we continue to ask simple questions.

"How many brothers and sisters do you have?"

Question after question, I find my hands naturally gliding as I carry on the conversation. Although I only have a year and a half of signing experience, compared with sixteen years of speaking English, signing feels completely natural. . . . I don't even have the urge to communicate by speaking.

By lunchtime, Jessica and I have become more than strangers. The nervous laugh we shared at the beginning of the day transforms into a burst of laughter about how boring her history teacher is. Between bites of peanut-butter sandwiches and sips of skim milk, we discuss our boyfriends.

"Wow, two years," she signs as I nod and smile. "I thought four months was a long time!"

"Did you see *Dawson's Creek* last night?" Jessica asks me. I nod my head.

"I can't believe he finally kissed her!" We both sign at the same time and giggle.

For some reason, I expected things to be different. I didn't expect to have so much in common with a girl who was randomly matched with me, especially since she was Deaf and I was hearing. I thought that we lived in such different worlds. But we don't. We have the same taste in clothes; we watch the same TV shows and share similar experiences about our boyfriends. We giggled together as all girls do and hugged each other good-bye when it was time for me to leave.

By the end of the day the butterflies were fast asleep. I guess they had a chance for that beauty sleep after all. ◙

Photo by Danielle Brown

The Bus Ride

by Melanie A. Rice

"I t's over! Thank goodness! Pedal to the metal!"

School was over and I was drained both mentally and physically. I sat in the very front of the bus because my desire to get home was overwhelming. Sitting in front makes you stand out like a shiny quarter in a pile of dull pennies that's doomed to be spent. Janie, the driver, tries to beat the awkwardness by striking the match and flame of conversation. I try to mind my manners and politely listen, but something about today's mindless drivel stuck with me. Today her conversation was worth listening to.

"My father's sick," she said to no one in particular. I could see the panic and fear in her eyes. It scared me. I had never seen her like this. She always had joy and smiles smeared across her heavily made-up face. She drove a lot of kids to and from school every day, and, to her, they were shimmering bars of gold, none more valuable than the other.

With a sudden change of attitude, I asked, "What's wrong with him?"

Her eyes glassy and her voice tight from fighting the tears, she responded, "Heart trouble." Her eyes lowered as she continued. "I've already lost my mom, and I just don't think I can stand losing him."

I couldn't respond. I was in shock. Afraid of her tears, she quickly closed the door, checked her bars of gold and gently pressed the accelerator. My heart ached for her.

I sat on the old, smelly seat thinking of the prolonged agony my own mother was thrown into when her father died. I saw how hard it was, and still is, for her. I wouldn't want anyone to go through that, even this forty-year-old bus driver.

Suddenly, I realized Janie wasn't *just* a bus driver; that was just her job. She had a whole world of family and concerns, too. I had never thought of her as anything but a driver. Suddenly, I felt very selfish. I realized I had only thought of people as far as what their purposes were in my life. I had never thought of them as people with lives and events of their own. My friends were just people in my life who comforted me when I needed it, just like I paid little attention to Janie because she was a bus driver. I had judged her by her occupation and brushed her off as insignificant.

For all I know, I'm just another person in someone else's world, and maybe not even significant. I shouldn't have been so selfish and self-involved. Everyone has places to go, people to see and schedules to keep. Understanding people is an art. 回

Driving with Dad

by Caty Simon

Your words are
threats submerged
in the soft notes of your tone
    my words make
grabs at your fatherly power
within their uncaring.
    We ride
staring at the
dust-flecked windshield
kissed by the apathetic afternoon
    sun.
    You try
to justify your actions
without admitting
you need to tell me the whys
of your paternal
plans.
    I snatch
the radio's storm-tinted dials
when hearing
my song.
    You, resenting
my daughterly control,

reach your hand
to tear my melodies
and listen to '60s
men sobbing about
perfect love.
  I scowl
at the rearview mirror
blocking your
  sight
looking at the ironic flower
behind my disgusted ear
and feeling
so H. Caulfield-y
driving with you.
Dad.

Photo by Alex Golub-Sass

Photo by Hadley Breed

Photo by Astride Noel

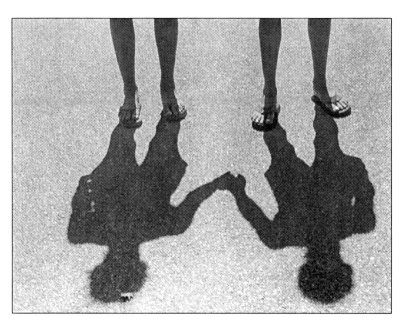

Photo by Emma Schofield

Photo by Sara Booth

Photo by Sara Elise Panzner

Photo by Michele Kulis

8 Bits of Memory

Photo by Jenn Christian

Here Comes the Bride

by Shea M. Seen

When I was seven, I married Michael Niccholl, a blond-haired boy in my second-grade class. It was a wedding at home, with a white dress, a blue suit, some plastic wineglasses filled with fruit punch, a turkey of sorts and a minister. I even had two bridesmaids. But before I go into more detail, I should probably explain why the wedding even took place, aside from the fact that we were madly in love.

I had a crush on Michael, and he liked me because I was the only one in our class who could spell his last name—Niccholl, not Nickel. He had surgery because the soft spot on his head never hardened, and he wore a bike helmet whenever he played outside. I thought he was the be-all and end-all of seven-year-olds, and when Halloween came around, I decided to make my move.

I was a bride for Halloween, with a white dress, veil, even a bouquet—and I was itching for a husband. Michael was Robin Hood and I decided he would do just fine. After gathering our minister—a girl named Lisa who was dressed as a friar—my two bridesmaids, who were dressed as Cinderella and a princess, and our wedding meal—a boy named Scott who had dressed up like a turkey—I went in search of my husband. I found him on the monkey bars and told him we were getting married and to hurry up because if you were late to your own wedding, your bride would hate you forever. Not given a choice, he reluctantly followed me to the picnic table, and the ceremony began.

Unfortunately, before we had said three words, the bell rang to end recess. I decided we would finish the ceremony at my house after school; I was determined to get married. Michael showed up on time with his groomsmen, our friends Andy and Tim. He was wearing a blue suit with a small flower on his lapel, no doubt put there by his mother. I got ready in my room. My baby-sitter gave Michael her sterling silver dolphin ring to use as a wedding band.

We all walked down the aisle—also known as our hall-way—and Lisa finished the ceremony. We decided it would be best if we shook hands instead of kissing. I mean, what if we got cooties or something? Afterward, we drank fruit punch from my plastic tea set and ate cookies. I changed my clothes, we went outside and played ball for a while and then Michael, Andy and Tim went home.

At the end of the school year, Michael moved to Ohio with his family. We were too young to do a very good job of keeping in touch, and so I lost contact with him. It's been almost ten years since I have seen or spoken to Michael Niccholl, but I think of the wedding often. I still have the ring and a picture of the two of us. I wonder if he ever thinks about me. I know I will probably never hear from him again, but I will never forget how to spell his name: N-I-C-C-H-O-L-L. ◘

Winter Mornings

by Jorge Quiñones

My fondest memory of my father is when I was a young child during the cold winter months in Texas. I would wake up feeling cozy in my soft bed, which was like living inside a freshly baked chocolate-chip cookie. Knowing that everything outside my bed was cold and frosty gave me chills.

My dad would enter my room to interrupt my dreams so I could get ready for school, saying, "*¡Hijo mío!* Rise and shine."

I would always try to weasel my way out of having to leave the bed, which never worked. As I'd stumble out of my refuge of blankets and sheets, my dad would sing a song he created just for me: "Stretch that body, stretch that body, make sure you don't hurt nobody," he would chirp. He had a voice that sounded like a train wreck, so it always made me laugh, and managed to get me up, too.

I still remember how the brisk winter air felt as I got out of bed and it wrapped around my body. And I can remember the texture of the floors as I slid across them in my one-piece pajamas with the footsies attached. Weary-eyed, I would chew my Fruity Pebbles while staring at cartoons on television. My dad would periodically poke his head into the kitchen, saying, "Hustle up, Son."

Eventually, I would finish breakfast, shuffle upstairs, fall into some clothes and haphazardly brush my teeth. I then stumbled back down the stairs, still sleepy and cold. It never failed—I don't know whether it was planned or just dumb luck—but I would always find my dad standing there in his jacket with mine in his hand. He never let me put my jacket on by myself, even after I had become quite good at it, and he would zip me up.

This part still causes the corners of my mouth to stretch from ear to ear. His hands always smelled of cologne. It wasn't a pungent, unpleasant odor, nor was it sweet. It was placid and safe. It said to me, *Son, I love you. I'll always take care of you and you'll never want for anything.* And to this day it has kept its promise.

My father's cologne represents everything he means to me. Hero, saint and dad are all expressed in that one scent. As he would zip up my jacket, I couldn't help but take in a deep breath. Maybe the sense of security it brought me as a child makes this such a fond memory, or maybe I'm just crazy. I know, however, that I would give almost anything to have that kind of relationship with my father again.

I hate the fact that I've put up walls between us for little reasons. He has never abused my mother or me, I have never gone a day without food, and he has always made sure I had the nicest clothes, the coolest toys, the smoothest bikes and the newest video games. His only fault, if you can call it that, has been that he loves me unconditionally and supports me in everything I do. When I fail, he encourages me, and when I disappoint him, he tells me how much he loves me.

I only hope that this memory I hold so dear and close to my heart will one day stop haunting the depths of my mind and become reality again. That will only happen when I demolish the walls I have unjustly built against the person who loves me the most. ▣

Photo by Jasmin Lehmann

I Love You

by Lynda Park

During my childhood, my grandmother was the one who tucked me in bed and never woke me up, unlike my mother, who would always wake me after eight hours yelling, "Get up! You've gotten enough sleep already!" My grandmother was an old lady, gray-haired, and wrinkly, with tiny, dark brown eyes that were so small they looked as though she couldn't see through them.

At her apartment, the scents of Korean food filled the air. She hustled around the small kitchen, cleaning any speck of dirt. It had to be perfect. Often my grandmother would feed me until a lead block settled in my stomach. "Eat more, eat more," she urged. Then she would offer me butterscotch, mint or cinnamon candy. Whenever we went anywhere together, she would always bring shelled peanuts without the thick, brown paper layer.

My grandmother's heart was bursting with love. "Come visit me," she would constantly say. And I would. Until I couldn't anymore.

Noisome and bustling hospitals replaced the cozy azure apartment. I remember visiting her, her skin now yellowish and soft. I laid my head on her lap, covered with white sheets, and cried. My grandmother stroked my smooth hair as my salty tears poured out, drenching the sheets, making them translucent.

After the hospital, she moved to convalescent homes, one after another. A prisoner in another world, my grandmother no longer kept herself busy in her kitchen, but instead spent her time in bed, eating, thinking and crying.

I knew she was in pain.

Sometimes I was annoyed with her, wondering why she had done this, making us worry. Such selfish thoughts!

Finally, the doctors prescribed morphine. One weekend, she asked to see my sister and me, but we didn't go. Days later, afraid that we might never see her again, we visited. She was asleep and breathing heavily. She seemed at peace and never looked more beautiful than at that moment.

I prayed for her, leaving her in the hands of God, and again I could feel burning tears filling my eyes. After my prayer, I kissed my grandmother on her tender cheek and said good-bye; she never knew I was there.

She never knew I was there.

Her dreams of seeing me go to college and marry and have kids were crushed. Her last memories of me were not what she wanted. If only she knew I was there. . . .

About nine hours after our visit, my grandmother died painlessly. I keep her with me always, glad she's not suffering, sad I won't be able to share my life with her. I know she's safe in heaven watching over me, even watching me write this now.

I want to say what I never got to say that last time: "I love you." ▣

The Kiss

by Thomas W. Sitzler

Kiss *her! Kiss her! KISS HER!* my mind screamed as we stood there outside her door. Hand in hand, smile to smile, eye to eye, we looked deep into each other's heart. My joints locked and my body froze as I put every ounce of courage into kissing her, but I could not move. I was stuck, like a paused image on a television screen. The night had been great—until now. I had to kiss her, I wanted to kiss her, I was going to kiss her. I took a step closer, leaned toward her and . . .

* * *

It was the first day of school and the halls were flooded with waves of students. I darted left and right, avoiding contact with other kids, and made my way to my first class. There she was. Katie's beauty surpassed the sunset. The bell rang and I quickly took a seat.

"Okay, class!" yelled the teacher. "Here are your assigned seats." She read the list and, to my amazement, I was right next to Katie.

This could be my chance, I thought. I leaned over the desk marked with years of graffiti and attempted to speak the words I'd rehearsed in my head for years. The smell of sweet flowers in spring titillated my nose. Preoccupied with her scent, I lost my balance and the desk fell over with a loud crash. All eyes peered at me and laughter escaped into the classroom. Katie giggled and smiled.

"Tom, is there a problem?" asked the teacher.

"N-no, ma'am," I said as I put my desk back in place. The bell rang and Katie disappeared.

* * *

The fiery red bowling ball rolled over the pins and broke my sleep. The next day had arrived and I had only one thought: Katie. I did my morning ritual and made my way to school. Across the hall from me was the angel who made my heart frolic. I walked over with a knot in my stomach and tapped her shoulder. "Hey, Katie," I said.

"Hey, Tom," she answered with a little anxiousness in her tone.

"Sooo . . . how's your day been?"

"Oh. Um, good."

"So, umm. Hey, Katie?"

"Yeah?"

"I-I-I was just wondering if, you know, if you w-w-weren't doing anything Friday maybe you'd, um, you'd want to, um," I stumbled over my words.

"Tom," she interrupted, "are you trying to ask me out or something?"

"Well, yeah," I responded grinning.

"Then the answer is yes," she said as the bell played its tune.

Hurray! I thought. Walking with a strut, I followed her into the classroom. A smile was glued to my face for the rest of the day.

* * *

Friday finally came, and I made my way to her house in my old Land Cruiser. Doused in Cool Water cologne, I popped a mint into my mouth and rang the doorbell. I stood for a while, listening to the voices on the other side. The door opened and there she stood, like an angelic sculpture.

"Ready?" she asked as the door closed behind her.

"I've been ready my whole life," I said with a half-smile. Her features tinted red and we got in my car. She sat there to my right, and as the moonlight hit her face, my heart sank deeper in love.

"Feel free to listen to whatever you like," I told her, pointing to the radio. She started searching the stations as if looking for a particular song. Then she stopped and Celine Dion came from the speakers. There is no other singer I would rather not listen to than her. To make matters more deafening, Kate starting singing off-key.

"Maybe we should just talk for a while," I said, but she frowned. "Or maybe not." I turned the radio back on and endured the torture. *Well, I have some qualities she wouldn't really like, so I guess I can bear it,* I consoled myself.

The night crept by as we ate dinner. We dove deeper into each other's eyes and discovered all the similarities between us. It was like she was my missing half. Everything about her was perfect (except the Celine Dion issue, but I could let that slide). She was an angel fallen from heaven. As she spilled out the words, I fell into a trance and was absorbed by her voice. Finally, dinner ended and the night at the movies began.

The movie was one of those chick flicks, but I guess it was all right. We walked outside and the night chilled our bodies. I placed my coat over her shoulders and put my arm around her waist. I smelled her golden locks that glittered with the moonlight and was reminded of spring flowers.

We made our way back through the winding roads as we listened to music (my choice, this time). We strolled down her walkway, holding hands and smiling. I stood there, looking deep into her eyes as the lights flickered behind us.

"Well, I had a fun time," she hinted in a small, sweet voice.

"So did I," I said. She stood there, waiting, and I knew why. My body froze for what seemed like hours but was actually only a few seconds. My mind yelled at me and I leaned forward in an attempt to kiss her good night. Our lips danced the waltz and our hearts sang the opera. What seemed like forever came to an end and she went inside. I stood there smiling, eyes closed, and recollected the night. *Thank you, Lord!* I said to myself as I returned to my car with lipstick on my lips. My car started with a roar and I drove home. ▣

Learning to Cook

by Destie Hohman

The heat as Mom opens the oven door makes me step back against the refrigerator. She slides the pan of cookies inside its depths while I look on.

"Mom, can I do it? I want to do it, Mom."

"When you're bigger, you can. I don't want you to get burned. Now, see how the oven's hot already? That's called preheating." She moves back to the table and sits down. I watch her for a moment. Her hair is lighter than mine. It slides over her shoulder, against her cheeks, slightly unbrushed. I think she is beautiful. Her hands move softly, working the dough on the table. They are pale and freckled, strong, but the skin lies over the bones like tissue. She lights a cigarette, and takes a drag. Everything she does is comfortable, familiar. She smells like smoke and Heaven Scent perfume, and when she's gone at night, I sneak her shirts into my bedroom to sniff as I fall asleep. I cannot imagine anything without her.

I pull a chair from the table and climb onto it. I cannot see the surface from the floor, but Luke will build me a stool, maybe, to stand on. Luke can do anything, I think. He fixes cars and stuff, and he fixes Mom, too, I guess. For Christmas, they gave me a tricycle that is painted metallic burgundy. They bought it at a yard sale for fifty cents, sanded and painted it with clearance spray paint. I love it just the same. I don't notice that they can't afford other things. It proves that Mom and Luke can do anything.

From my chair, I help Mom. We take pieces of piecrust and make a triangle out of them. Mom sprinkles on cinnamon sugar, but she won't let me. I am upset, because I know I could do it.

"Mom, Mom, let me do it. Let me do it!" Mom finally hands the jar to me; I slowly spill the grains across the table and cooking sheet. I think she is smiling.

The dough is soft and squishy. It sticks to my fingers when I roll it up (big end to small end), but that's okay. The sugar is grainy when I lick it off my hands. The house smells warm and good from the crescents in the oven. I eat the dough when Mom isn't looking.

The kitchen is my favorite room. It has a long, skinny table at one end and a sink at the other. I know that the Formica counter is white with funny green flecks, even though I'm not tall enough to see it. The refrigerator is a color Mom calls avocado, and the stove is pink. I like it. There is one window at the sink end. Later I will learn to whistle at that window, looking out at the neighbor's yard. The curtains are sheer and white, with little cotton baubles hanging at the edges. They are ugly. I look out the window at the rain and want to live in the kitchen forever.

On other days, it is sunny when Mom and I cook. We are making fried chicken to take camping. It is Memorial Day or the Fourth of July. Or Labor Day. They all run together, but they are camping days, and they are in the summer. I like holidays a lot. Last year on Valentine's Day, Luke brought me a white dress with blue flowers for no reason at all. He brought Mom chocolate candy and a card. Camping holidays are the best, though. We go with my aunt and uncle, and I swim with no clothes on with my aunt and mom. At night we sit around the fire, and I climb into the tent to sleep while they play cards in the lantern-light.

Fried chicken is hard to make. Mom asks me to stir while she goes to the bathroom. I stir for a long time, until I get tired. Some falls out of the bowl. I wipe it up with my fingers and stick it in my mouth. It is awful. I climb off the chair and onto the counter. I open the cupboard door and look at the jars. I pull out the one labeled p-e-p-p-e-r and sprinkle black flecks into the batter. I stir more, careful not to spill any. Then I add more and stir more, until the batter is full of black specks. I think it looks nice, much better than the smooth white batter. When Mom comes back, I tell her right away but she doesn't think it is very pretty.

"Destie!" she says loudly. When Mom cooks, she makes everything from white cards, reading the whole thing before and during cooking. The cards tell her what to do. I didn't see any card talking about pepper, but I didn't look either. If it tastes good, I don't think it matters that much. But Mom likes to know how much to put into things.

When we are camping that night, we eat cold chicken with lots of pepper. I think it is good, but no one else takes seconds, probably because they see how much I like it. Probably my favorite camping food is s'mores. I like all the dirt and things that get in the food when we camp. I used to peel my apples and roll them in the sand before I ate them, because the kids in the neighborhood thought that was gross. I didn't like them. The kids, I mean. The apples were fine.

Mom and I cook chocolate-chip cookies together also. And pumpkin pie. I don't like raw pumpkin pie. But raw cookies are good. I eat as much as I can before Mom catches me. I like the way the sugar grinds in my teeth when I chew it. I like them hot, too, when the chocolate burns my tongue and the milk tastes extra cold because of it. Most foods are good raw, especially desserts and stuff. I also like Jell-O when it's hot and sort of slippery. It's good to suck off the wooden spoon and tastes kind of limey.

For the rest of my life, one of my favorite things will be cooking with my mom. We don't do it a lot, but I like it. When I'm older, I'll want to do it on my own, to prove that I can, I guess. But later, I will want to cook with Mom to have her teach me how—to be a child again—because this time is so perfect. To have someone who knows tell me just how to do it, how much to add and for how long, so that there is no guessing and things always come out just right. It won't be the same as it is now. Sometimes, I won't want to help. I will just want to watch, to see the way she moves, stirring and pouring. Maybe she will think that I don't want to be with her, or maybe I don't want her helping me. I will just love the sight of her, so familiar and warm. There is nothing better than cinnamon crescents with Mom on a rainy day. ◙

His Gift

by David Pease

The room was a shared universe.
I had my bureau,
My side of the closet,
My Legos and my action figures.
He had the top bunk,
The left side of the closet.
He had the rule of age.

He was bigger so I listened,
I followed, I obeyed,
Most of the time.

My brother's imagination
Was bigger than I could imagine.
He saw things, sees things
That I couldn't, can't.
Some he shared,
Some he kept to himself.

Those that he shared
Influenced me and changed the
Way I think so that I am just
Discovering their effects now.

He once shared with me
A part of his imagination
That I wish he hadn't.
"The big, dark, scary closet next
To our bed is filled with monsters,
Vampires, ghosts and demons."

My imagination filled in the blanks.
I never slept facing the closet.
Ever,
Again.

One day he turned our bed
Into a fishing boat
Floating over the massive, white-tipped
Waves of an ocean all our own.
Other days it was a raft,
Drifting over a sea of lethal lava,
The carpet.

Today it became a boat.
The magnet tied with a shoestring,
Our rescue line.
The Matchbox cars,
Sprinkled over the carpet,
Our desperate crew, thrown overboard
Struggling to keep their heads above
Water.

Hours we spent tossing the lifeline
To crew members, who
Were very picky about how
The line was tossed to them.
If it wasn't just right
They would let go or,
Not even try to reach the line
At all.

After the crew was safe aboard,
We would be off,
To the jungle in the backyard,
The Egyptian caves in our basement,
Or the torture chamber in the attic.

Without him I wouldn't have had
The boat, the jungle, the caves.
At the time I didn't realize
The greatness of these gifts.

Photo by Sarah Roberto

Just One Ride

by Rachel Anderson

y dad was the coolest. When I was five, he was who I wanted to be. There was no one out there like him.

He had a love for motorcycles and I had a love for Barbie's pink Corvette, but soon my love would change. I would hear his bike from all the way down the street; it sounded like a thousand drums beating at once. Then he would come soaring down our driveway on his purple Harley, while I eagerly watched from my upstairs window. I always wished that one day I would be strapped to the back of his bike, holding tightly with the wind blowing in my face and the smell of the freshly cut grass tickling my nose as we rode.

Of course, I was only five, and my mother would have gone crazy if she had seen me on the back of his bike. "It's not safe for a little girl, Frank, that's why!" was always her response when he would say, "C'mon, just one ride, she'll love it. I'll be careful, I swear." And I certainly would have loved it. I prayed and prayed for that day she would let me have a ride. But she never gave in, so instead I'd sit up in my room watching him take off into the night on his beautiful bike.

Then it happened—I got my chance. I was allowed to

ride the bike. Well, that's what Dad told me. He said Mommy didn't mind, but I probably shouldn't tell her. It would be our little secret. I grabbed the helmet, threw it on and was ready to take off into the sunset. He began to rev the engine; it sent chills up my spine. My dream had finally come true. I was thinking of nothing but how amazing it felt to be on the back of my dad's bike. That night, I felt as though I were on top of the world.

Then, one night, my parents went out for dinner. My mom was petrified of the bike, so they took the car. As they were leaving, I jumped on Dad's back and gave him a giant bear hug. He said, "Good-bye, I love you," and then his famous "Be good."

Later that night, I knew something was wrong. I woke at 3:15 A.M. and went into my parents' room to sleep with them, but they weren't there. I felt a wave of panic sweep through my body as I searched the house. I was in the middle of an anxiety attack.

Then the worst news I had ever heard hit me. There I was, a child standing in the kitchen while three of my aunts tried to explain to me that Mommy was sick and Daddy wouldn't be coming home, not today or any day. They explained that there had been a terrible accident and Daddy was up in heaven. I just stared at them, motionless, not knowing what to say.

All I wanted to do was jump on his bike and ride away, far away. Tears didn't come; I gazed into the swollen and bloodshot eyes of my aunts without expression. I felt lost and wondered if I'd ever be found. I wanted him back so we could ride again, so I could see the passion in his eyes just once more as we took off on his love—his bike.

So, now, at seventeen, I hold a secret in my heart. I look back and realize how wonderful Dad was and what a shame it is that I only had a chance to be with him for five years. Every time I see a motorcycle fly by me into the night, I think of him. And I know that he is somewhere where he can ride his bike day and night, waiting for me to join him so that we can take off into the night together, once more. ▣

Shortcut Home

by Cynthia Oquendo

y family took a lot of road trips back to New York, usually in Dad's tiny old Dodge. If you had seen that car—there were still a few around back then—you'd point and laugh. But all those years ago, they weren't that old, and it ran well enough to get us past the state border.

It had been an especially long trip for me, a nine-year-old girl, and even longer for my thirty-something parents. Our band of tired, angry family members was on the brink of homicide as we pulled into a gas station, a welcome release from the perpetual boredom of the car ride. The smell of gasoline and cigarette smoke mixed with the various odors of my sisters' feet making me nauseous. I stuck my head out the window for air (not that it helped) and searched halfheartedly for something interesting. She was coming my way.

I waited for Dad to disappear into the store, then whispered excitedly to Mom who looked up from her crocheting, fixating on the apparition I was pointing out. It was Jessica Sweat, a close friend of mine I hadn't seen since kindergarten. Now in fourth grade, I measured our separation in decades.

Mom flagged down Jessica with that high-pitched

voice only a mother has. The tiny girl looked up warily, took a step, then stopped. I shouted and she, probably more out of confusion than recognition, came toward us.

It was a warm morning, but Jessica had her hands deep in the pockets of a ratty jacket. As she came closer, she cast her head down. There was no bounce in her step. She didn't even smile, but ever so slightly simpered when our eyes met. Of course, I didn't notice any of this; I was simply beaming to see her. Here was Jessica, the girl who cried when I cut my waist-length hair, the person who staunchly defended me in a game of "Who Stole the Cookie from the Cookie Jar," and the friend who had disappeared the summer before first grade. Some part of this earlier, carefree Jessica was gone, obvious even to a naive young child like me.

"Jessica, hey!" I waved.

"Hi, Cynthia," she called back. She had recognized me. "Where've you been? I never see you anymore."

"I moved to Connecticut." *Didn't she know?* I wondered. *Wait, how could she have?*

"Really?" She thought for a second. I don't know if she was accepting a difficult truth, or just trying to remember where Connecticut was. "I thought you just went to Mt. Carmel," she conceded. Our Lady of Mt. Carmel was a private Catholic school a town away.

"I was there for three months. I didn't like that school."

"Now we live in Danbury," Mom interjected.

"Oh," Jessica sighed. "I've never heard of Danbury."

"Neither had I," I admitted. Conversation was reaching its anticlimax, since what do two nine-year-olds have to catch up on? If a playground were nearby, it would have been like nothing had changed, but now only an eaves-dropping mother was in the vicinity. "We're back because my parents have stuff to do with our old condo. Where were you going?"

"This is my shortcut home."

Mom couldn't restrain herself. "You were walking home alone? Don't your parents think that's dangerous?"

"Not really," she said, sullenly. "I live pretty close, and my father's home—he doesn't work. He doesn't really want me around when his friends are over anyway." She was nine, remember. A child doesn't learn the art of covering up by nine.

"Your father?" Mom asked.

"Uh-huh."

Then a curious thing happened. Both Jessica and Mom clammed up. They turned their heads away, fiddled with their clothes and looked uncomfortable. But it was a nagging sort of uncomfortable, like a fly crawling on your arm that keeps returning no matter how many times you flick it away. In all my innocence I felt like they had shared something without me, and I mentally accused Mom of trying to steal my friend.

"I missed you," I said.

Jessica smiled, genuinely. "I missed you, too. But I should get home now. I'm sorry."

"That's all right. I'll see you soon." More of my childhood innocence; I never saw Jessica again.

"Okay," she said. "Bye, Cynthia. Bye, Mrs. Oquendo."

And with that she turned and left, walking at the same defeated pace as before. Mother and I watched. This conversation hadn't lasted more than two minutes, but the weight of the subtext of her every word seemed to drag the morning down. And I didn't understand any of it.

"Is she all right?" I asked Mom.

Mom said something about Jessica living in a bad environment, having a hard life ahead of her—that sort of thing. I just thought Jessica had had a bad day; I didn't grasp the concept of "hard life," and couldn't spell "environment" let alone know what it meant. All it did was make me worry about her, and I grew frustrated on the car ride home trying to figure out how to help. But maybe that was the point.

When Dad came back, glancing in the direction of my quickly vanishing friend, he asked, "Who was that?"

I sat back between my two sisters, who had slept through it all, and answered, "I don't know." ◙

One of a Kind

by Brooke Cooper

here is a piece of paper
just a piece of paper to the untrained eye,
but you have an imaginative soul and
a curious mind and you know what lies inside

one magnificent snowflake
a one-of-a-kind gem that comes once in a
lifetime and melts perfectly on your nose

a grassy field at the end of a long road
with hay bales to the sky and a perfect
hill to roll down and a perfect tree to climb

a hundred sunny days since the first one
that we shared and went swimming in the
lakes and fishing in my tub

a million different crayons as special as
the last, that have colored our letters
and our posters at four in the morning

one great wondrous big dipper that's
perfect from anywhere
but breathtaking from half-court

a billion old songs that always sound
better in our off-key duet and an equal
amount of poses to any available mirror

all the tears of frustration and petty
words over checkers but infinitely as
much laughter from things only funny
to the young at heart or absent in mind . . .

countless talks of all our past wishes and
desires our discussions where we differ
in religion, attitude, or mascara on a male

the imprints of our noses mine slightly
larger on the windows of the corner café

all the rain clouds we've danced under and
equally as many remarks we've endured . . . but
we've endured together

all this is ours contained in this piece
of paper time will take the paper
and for some the memory and eventually
us but what is written in the words
is here forever, like our souls . . .
you me
our friendship

Will You Remember Me?

by Atara Schimmel

I still remember the day. It was the beginning of freshman year. The first day of Latin class. I had attended a different junior high so I didn't know many people. I remember looking around at all the faces, wondering which ones would become my friends.

I dropped out of Latin the next day; my schedule was too demanding. A year and a half later, she told me, "I couldn't understand why you were smiling so much. Every time I turned to look at you, you smiled." In that Latin class she was just another stranger, a part of the crowd.

In English class she was still another stranger with a name. And then, somewhere in the middle of the year, somehow, she crossed the room and sat next to me. Since then, we sat together. Now, she's one of my best friends.

I really love spending time with Liz. She lets things flow by her, lapping past and then she snatches little bits and they touch her, softly.

Now, I can look into her sparkling blue eyes, those coral-like eyes. They've got white speckles in them and a little ring of yellow around the pupil. I can look into

her eyes and know what lies beyond them. She's no
longer a stranger. How does one break the barrier? When
did we reach the point where we could open up, could
cry with each other, could tell each other how important
the other is?

*Like throwing little pieces of bread into a pond, throw-
ing little pieces of me into her. She accepts or doesn't, but
she doesn't judge and neither do I, we just share. . . .*

My memories of us will be light, silent memories. I'll
remember us walking through the night, bumping against
each other and sharing ourselves until our words jumbled,
intertwined. I'll remember us twirling in the mud, barefoot
. . . flying through the air on the swings. . . .

*I get engulfed in life. I let it touch me, I let it hurt me.
She lets it be.*

*I remember our little treks into town; we never went
anywhere but we always had fun.*

*She's very sensitive and picks up on things here and
there, poking and lightly pulling like a child pulls a loose
string out of your coat.*

I'll remember the time I sat in her room, waiting for
her math lesson to be over. She gave me her diaries and
poetry, leaving me to read them. I remember the telephone conversation we had when I came back from my
ten-day stay in Israel. She told me that she had cried and
couldn't study because she was constantly worried about
me. I laughed hysterically. I felt so loved; someone had
worried just about me. It felt wonderful, and I loved her
all the more for being able to tell me how much she
needed me, how much I meant to her.

Next year I'll be going to Israel to study. She'll

probably take it the hardest of all my friends. I remember the tennis courts, Liz and I sprawled on the pavement in the sun. She asked me, "Will you remember me?" I laughed. The question was so sensitive, so innocent and sweet, the answer so obvious. Or the time on the phone when she said, "Sometimes I wonder what I give to you." *Liz flows. She taught me to take life more lightly. To protect myself from its sting. To let the little ugly things just flow by into the past.*

When I think of next year, I already miss her. It's true—I can't wait to leave, to move on. But as I move on, make new friends, maybe even get my first boyfriend, I'll never forget that she's still there, waiting for me, eager to pop back into my life. And I love her for this, for her honesty, for the warmth I see in her eyes. I can't wait to introduce her to my friends in Israel—to share with her everything that makes me happy. ◙

Photo by Alex Marquez

Loving Hands

by Beth Bednarz Pruski

Mothers are usually a very significant part of childhood memories. My earliest recollections are unique. In my mind I see pictures of her hands moving gracefully in front of her, forming letters, words and sentences I could not yet understand. My mother is deaf.

As a child, I doubted and questioned that she could not hear. Often, for my own proof, I would stand behind her and scream. Not once did she flinch or whirl around to scold me. After I realized that my mother was different, I began to notice things other mothers could do that mine couldn't. She could not hear the radio or television or answer the phone without the help of her hearing aid. These everyday activities are often taken for granted.

At a young age I was exposed to the adult world because I provided ears for my mother so she could communicate with the world. I always had difficulty trying to assume responsibility. How seriously does one take a six-year-old on the telephone calling for her "mommy" and arranging doctors' appointments? And so, I endured the constant struggle of being taken seriously.

As I grew older, I discovered ways to use the situation to my advantage. How easy it was at thirteen to walk out of a room after an argument with her and say horrible things to which she wouldn't respond. Unfortunately, but honestly, such a habit is not easy to break, although I now feel badly about these actions.

More than once I have felt guilt, but the hardest emotion to suppress is shame. Simple elementary-school friendships do not require an explanation that your mother is handicapped, a word I still hesitate to use in describing her. But, for many people, *handicapped* sadly is a word they cannot see beyond. I have found that true friends accept not only you, but your family, too. They are also the ones who do not even notice the effort they need to make to speak slowly and look at my mom when they talk, since she has an extraordinary talent to lipread, and they barely notice when asked to repeat things. I myself do not always have these qualities because I still become frustrated when I cannot communicate as easily as I would like.

At age five, I learned basic sign language and very often, to reinforce a point I was trying to make, I spoke and signed simultaneously. I still hesitate to sign in public. In a restaurant or store, people stare at anyone signing. It has taken a lot of self-confidence to overcome the stares, and I now feel a sense of pride being able to communicate in a special way. I have learned that many people don't know that someone can be handicapped yet carry on a life that is barely different from their own.

I have overcome many obstacles to accept the mother with whom I have been blessed, and I honestly would not trade her for any other, although at age seventeen, there are times I think I would like to. ◉

9 Different Connections

Photo by Dyani Jensen

A Letter to Cupid

by Rachel Roth

Dear Cupid,

Most people remember the first time they said (or heard) those three magic words. Exchanging *I love you* is a memorable event. Well, not for me. *I love you* has become one of those hackneyed phrases. I hear it countless times each day—from my friends, on television, on the radio.

The first time a boy told me that he loved me was probably in fifth grade—some note passed carefully so the teacher wouldn't notice. And, as I recall, it did not even spell out the words. Probably more like a picture of an eye next to a heart next to a "U." Very special. And being a boy-crazy preteen, I am sure I responded with an even more elaborate heart; you know, the kind with arrows.

By eighth grade, the *I love you*'s matured a bit. Then, the cool thing to do was tell your boyfriend of two weeks (or two days) you loved him; this usually happened about halfway through the Friday night movie that your fifty friends religiously attended. So I guess I was sitting through a romantic scene of *Wayne's World 2* when I heard those magic words again. Excellent!

As a seventeen-year-old, I really hate to admit that *I*

love you still does not mean much. One boyfriend told me he loved me for the first time in the hallway right before biology. Pardon me for not bursting with joy. I began dating a guy who was my best friend for two years; we had said "I love you" about a million times. Once we were an official couple, the words sounded like they always had: monotonous.

The Internet introduces a whole new twist. Whenever I receive mail from friends, acquaintances or random characters who always seem to be online, the letters are signed *Love always* or *Love ya,* or my personal favorite *Luv Ya Tonz*. I admit it: I am guilty, too.

I think we need a new word, the kind that means I love you as a friend. It makes sense; I really do love my friends. But it is not the stereotypical music-playing, running-through-the-fields-toward-the-love-of-my-life love. More like here's-some-e-mail, I-will-call-you-later love.

So, that's my request. Thanks for listening; hopefully you can find a solution.

Love always, Rachel 回

Don Juan, Goldfish

by Lisa Kelly

I don't hate many things, but yogurt and fish are two exceptions. I'm still not crazy about yogurt, but fish are a bit different. The story of one hero comes from the short yet inspiring life of my goldfish, Don Juan.

The summer before my sister left for college, her friend decided to buy me some fish to keep me company. She invited me to go with her to the pet store to pick out the perfect fish. Naturally, I searched for the cheapest, most healthiest-looking ones. We spent two dollars and left with five goldfish.

As we put them in their tank at home, we made bets about which fish would live the longest. We both selected a vibrant and lively orange goldfish. I identified a sickly white one as the fish who would die first. Boy, was I wrong.

I wasn't very good at taking care of fish. I didn't know when or how much to feed them, and changing their water was a chore. The first fish died a day after its arrival. Surprisingly, it was not the sickly white one. Day by day, I lost the other fish until just the white one remained. I figured it would only be a matter of time before he hit the toilet as well.

Months passed, and the white fish was still alive. I grew quite fond of him, looking forward to when I would feed him or watch him swim in his bowl. I soon noticed, however, that he had some problems.

I would drop a few small flakes of food and watch as they rested on the water's surface. Don Juan swam to the surface and began to eat . . . the water. I watched this for some time and came to the conclusion that my beloved fish had some type of eye problem. The only flakes he could see were the biggest ones that only came in brand-new packages of fish food. I decided that Don Juan had inadvertently gone on a severe diet, some type of massive fast.

It finally hit me that I should go to the pet store and buy a new package of fish flakes to help my visually impaired friend. By rationing the large flakes and having Don Juan follow my finger across the water to smaller ones, his eating habits improved drastically.

When he was almost a year old, my fish and I experienced quite a traumatic adventure. Bringing him into the bathroom, I planned to transfer him back into his freshly cleaned bowl. Having performed this transfer many times before, I had become an expert. I drained most of the dirty water until Don was left with just a little, then immediately shifted him into his humble abode. I hit him a bit too hard, propelling him into a nearby trash barrel.

Completely stunned and overcome with shock, I covered my flapping friend with a tissue, figuring he was close to death. I ran out of the bathroom, shaking. I returned his bowl to my room, thinking I would no longer need it.

My mother came home five minutes later. A frantic mess, I told her the story.

"Is he still in the trash?" she asked, heading toward the bathroom. I couldn't watch. I stayed far from the crime scene, praying my mother could revive Don.

I heard her shriek with excitement that he was still alive! I told her to put him in the bowl, forgetting I had put it back in my room. Using logical reasoning and quick action, my mother threw the fish into the toilet bowl. At this point, I ran to see my friend, but he had disappeared. How many places could a fish hide in a toilet?

With much luck, my mother located the missing fish and safely returned him to his bowl. I looked at his white body. Blood spots lined his fins and gills. He resembled the Polish flag more than Flipper. I figured he'd die, suffering from post-traumatic stress disorder. Once again, he proved me wrong.

This accident brought us closer together. I took extra-special care of Don and even planned to get him a larger tank with fun fish decorations for Christmas. Unfortunately, my plans were altered.

I awoke for school one winter morning. Turning on the light to get dressed, a black spot on my white rug caught my attention. Bending to investigate, I realized it was Don Juan.

Once again, I was a mess. I ran downstairs, screaming for my dad. He made the trek to my room and identified the body. "Oh yeah, he's cooked," Dad said. I heard the toilet flush.

I told all my friends the horrifying story as soon as I got to school. They laughed and expressed their condolences. I brushed it off, but midway through the day it hit me: My fish, my friend, was dead.

An autopsy was never conducted. Suicide cannot be ruled out; the place on the rug where Don landed was quite some distance from his bowl that sits on the top shelf of a small bookcase. The fall alone may have killed him. No one knows exactly how long he flapped on the rug after suffering severe head trauma. My mom thinks the cat had some role in this mystery, but I can still picture Don's body in my head and I am positive there were no claw marks. Also, the cat has never been very fond of seafood products.

My fish is a hero. He overcame adversity; it's not easy being a white goldfish. He overcame visual difficulties and an eating disorder. He survived one brush with death. I do miss him; I've never gotten so much enjoyment out of twenty-four cents before or since. His death was quite a shock, as was his life. Don Juan might not have done much for others, but he broadened my appreciation for one thing I had previously scorned. I'm still working on yogurt. 回

Photo by Ryan Healy

Calling a Friend

by Mallory Ho

*As you approach me, the world encloses and separates us
    from everything.
The sun seems to lose its grace and luster.
The ground feels as though it were not there; a figment of
    the imagination now
escaping beneath my feet.
My body is no longer a part of me.*

*As the tears begin to stream down your face, my entire
    body begins to tremble.
A thousand thoughts race across my mind and you are
    at the center of each
and every one of them.
Not a single word is spoken as you attempt to push a
    fraudulent smile through your wet face.*

*As I search my mind for a word of comfort, I reach the
    perfect resolution.
I offer you my most sincere smile and you receive it with
    a look of relief.
I walk up beside you with open arms and you shyly
    fall into them.*

*The tears are now flowing from your eyes as your sobs are
pouring from your soul.*

*I calm you with my gentle hushes as a salty teardrop
escapes from my damp, restrained eyes.*

*I know I cannot solve your problems; I can only stay by
your side throughout your time of trial.*

*As silence falls upon us like the shadow of the night,
the world stands still in our moment of reflection.*

*I feel like we are forever protected from the world
and all of its evils.*

You are safe now and that is all that matters.

*I cannot help but break down in tears when the soft words
are released from
your no longer shivering lips . . .*

"Thank you for being my friend."

Rebels Six

by Christopher Gubelmann

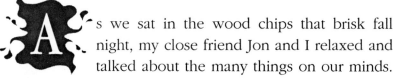

s we sat in the wood chips that brisk fall night, my close friend Jon and I relaxed and talked about the many things on our minds. We had been best friends all our lives, and this conversation was a time of reflection and learning.

The wood-chip pile was in the neighborhood leaf dump, a place we had spent much of our childhood building forts, riding dirt bikes, and just being away from everyone. The dump was our kingdom.

We began discussing all the things we used to do. We remembered walking into high school for the first time together, and even our years of middle school. The more we talked, the more we realized how fast the time had gone by that had seemed to take forever at the time. Our neighborhood had been perfect, with the dump, school, a BMX course and even a golf course where we would play Army.

"Jon, do you remember when people told us they would love to be our age again, and we couldn't figure out why?" We finally realized what adults had been telling us, and how we had taken our youth for granted. As our conversation continued, I became angrier and more frustrated. I kept wishing I could stop the hands of time. We had finally realized how lucky we were to have such close friends, and so many great places and opportunities to have fun.

For years we had dreamed of being older. We always had fun at parties, but we never totally enjoyed ourselves. We always wanted to be the older kids who threw the parties. We wanted to be able to tell the younger kids what we did when we were their age.

Now we were finally living out our wishes. For a second it felt great to realize that our older brothers were no longer around, and we were now the oldest. Now we drove cars, we were looked up to, we threw the parties and we were admired by the younger kids.

Then this great feeling was crushed when we thought about the next year. Jon was going to be a United States Marine, Ogar was going upstate, Casper would be a hundred miles away in college, Reed and Dart would be working, and I would be at school. It was our last year together. Eventually time would reap our youth and we would become men.

It was at that point that Jon and I vowed to live our lives to the fullest. To live the moment for what it was, and to enjoy it, not just because it leads to the next. Although we had experienced many great times, each second that we had wasted would never return, and next year the Rebels Six would just be six rebels, each on his own path to manhood. And although we will all be friends forever, our time living and growing up together is going by fast.

The more I think about that night, the more I wish I could gather all the kids who want to grow up and make them see how they should cherish every moment. So many don't understand how lucky they are.

This is not to say that college won't be fun, but as we sat that night, I learned to appreciate what I have and to live every moment for all that it is worth. ◎

Photo by Patrick Michael Baird

The Date

Fiction by Sierra Black

We missed the beginning of the movie. It doesn't matter. The floors are just as sticky, the lobby just as red, and stale Twizzlers still cost two dollars a box. Ticket stub clutched in one sweaty palm, my fingers wrapped loosely in yours, we pick our way through spilled soda and congealed popcorn, scramble over people's knees into a corner, dim light from a niche in the wall spilling on your profile.

It is a bad movie, high-budget Hollywood glitter, full of bad actresses with ten-inch waists and bad actors with twenty-inch biceps. We laugh when the heroine dies; no one else thinks it is funny.

The movie ends and we float out, flowing with the faceless crowd to the glowing red exit signs. Alone in this herd, me dancing like I was in a sunbeam, I later can't remember what we talked about. Words are like masks to cover the silent connection between us. Outside the night is fresh, crisp warmth like you only get in wintertime: sharp black sky, bright stars like broken strands of Christmas lights lying on a crumpled black velvet party dress. The night air kisses my hands, my cheeks, my hair. I dance ahead across the pavement like a broken piece of night. Standing by the car you catch me in a close hug, slow like syrup, a frozen moment, no sound, no breath. You laugh and let me go. I bounce away like soap bubbles, everything light and nonsense again. Conversation resumes like it hadn't stopped. What were we talking about? I start the car.

We fall to riding in comfortable silence, the road stretching out ahead like a black silk ribbon. The wheel under my fingers feels strong and solid. The driver's seat curves to my body. The night silence has a strong calm. I feel my heartbeat mimicking the flash and fade pattern of street lamps; no headlights blur my windshield, alone on the road. Each turn of my wrist; each breath that moves my rib cage. You are speaking again, in a low voice that only deepens our silence. Am I hungry? Chinese food? Take a right at the lights; there's a good restaurant up there.

Cheesy red paper lanterns dangle overhead, Friday night karaoke in the bar where all the drinks come with pink umbrellas. The waiter comes to seat us, a pimply-faced kid who looks more Swedish than Chinese. We sit in nonsmoking, an unfamiliar treat. I think about smoking, about all my food tasting like ashes, about kissing someone who smokes. . . . Your voice interrupts before my thoughts go any further. I flash a grateful smile and lean over your shoulder to examine the menu. All the crazy Chinese names, five kinds of chop suey. What is chop suey? We decide to order spare ribs and some sort of gooey vegetable dish. The waiter brings us stale dinner rolls and dirty water, but we don't care enough to send them back. Instead we do magic tricks with the salt shaker until our food comes, and the spare ribs make us laugh—they're hot pink like a Slurpee but we eat them anyway and the juice runs down my chin. I have to ask for more napkins; the waiter gives me an evil glare, so you say we should stiff him on the tip, but when the bill comes we leave him three dollars just the same. Crack open my fortune cookie. By crazy chance we both pull the same fortune from the broken crust of cookie—"You will soon find romance with an old friend." We joke about it, but suddenly the air is heavy again, thick and much too sweet like pure maple syrup, until I blush a little, and you dissolve the unsaid stickiness with little bits of thrown fortune cookie that stick in my hair.

Outside with the odd semisweet taste of fortune cookies hovering on my breath, the bright embrace of night, wild gold and white electric lights glaring like a thousand shards of broken glass, like a flashlight shone against broken beer bottles in the far corner of a parking lot, a million tiny flames in that always dark corner as the night watchman makes his rounds with a halogen lantern. The lights look like that, and we stand a minute by the car, leaning back against the aerodynamic curve, looking breathless up into the sky. The night so fresh and vital, our night does not seem over.

We cruise around a bit, weaving through the electric storefront maze. The juicy white lights of a laundromat suck us in—signs in the wide pane windows: *Seventy-five cents a load. Open twenty-four hours.* I pull in and turn the key; we race to reach the soda machine, slamming together as we both jam our quarters in, splitting a root beer. I sit up on a washer, kicking my heels against the mustard lacquer side, cool metal shivers on the backs of my thighs. I take a long sip of root beer, feel the tingly, jumpy bubbles run into my belly, carrying off that faint lingering fortune-cookie flavor.

We are alone, and every sound seems loud, everything surreal under the harsh fluorescent bulbs. Cool clink of metal, the can set down on the washer next to mine, your cool hands on my knees. You catch my eyes and I'm breathing maple syrup again, looking at you in this frozen silence, trapped in this dream place that isn't really anywhere except you and me and a mustard-colored washing machine.

This time the silence doesn't break, doesn't fall to the floor and shatter into a million little silent pieces for some surreal fluorescent janitor to sweep up later. No, some-how I don't drop it, even when you kiss me, when I feel your soft mouth on mine in the maple-syrup silence, and realize, your tongue hot on my lips, that I must have leaned forward to kiss you, and that I'm kissing you back, and that I'm slipping. . . . We both laugh as I tumble off the washer into your arms, knocking us both off balance, into a crazy spin around the laundromat. I cling to your neck and we kiss again.

Later on I drop you off, promise to call. Driving home alone with this strong black night, I smell your skin on my hair, taste you in my mouth, and smile, the kind of deep, secret smile that no one ever understands, that way you see people smiling when they are remembering something soft and good and secret. ▣

Trainmate Jack

by Beth M. Putnam

This is a poem to my trainmate Jack
whom I met on a cloudy Wednesday
as I stepped on the crowded train.
Collapsing in the first vacant seat,
I smiled at the stranger next to me.
I carried fatigue and luggage,
dreading the six-hour ride.
You offered me potato chips
and conversation with hopeful eyes.
Told me of regrets and wishes—
wondering how eighty years slipped by
so quickly
and the next you knew
you had lost a wife and son.
Asked me with a wide grin to marry you
and travel the world by your side.
"Be happy you're eighteen," you said.
"Live every day to its fullest."
The ride ended, we stepped off
and into the station,
looking to others like a girl and her grandfather,
but we were friends.
Through the door we could see

the hurried pace of the city,
people rushing to speed up their lives.
We stood together,
side by side.
Two people traveling alone for the first time.
A wave good-bye and a promise
to remember your advice,
to take in each day
as it comes.
So I write this poem
in thanks and hope to you, my trainmate Jack.

Stiles

by Emily N. Trask

On the train ride to Chicago I met a man named William G. Stiles, or so said his nametag. I met him rather by accident. He was joking loudly with some kids, telling them that he was traveling farther than they were. Turning around to see what the commotion was all about, I saw him. As I peeked my nose over the back of my seat, the ruckus turned to me and flashed a smile. "And where are you going?" he asked softly.

"Colorado," I replied.

"Ha," he said, "and I'm going farther than you!"

This book of knowledge was very eager to share his experiences with everyone he met. Curly grey hair puffed out from underneath an ancient, dusty, navy blue beret. Very seldom did he remove his cap, for it was one of his prized possessions. Probably a token of one of his many adventures or maybe a souvenir from the navy that he'd been in for thirty years. That was, and is, his trademark; everything else was just for fun.

A map perhaps of his life was imprinted on his face. Every centimeter of his face was covered with lines. Between his old lips and tired teeth sat a piece of wood. This toothpick belonged there and did not move even for a cough or yawn. That was his sign to show the world he was pleased with himself and comfortable wherever he went. The stick added character to his ramblings, giving them meaning.

This self-contained man carried all his belongings with him, never having to worry that he would forget anything, although once or twice I noticed that he seemed to lose a piece of paper or other small things that meant the world to him. Hanging from his waist was a large pouch with the word *Rossignol* across the front. The sagging bag contained everything one would need to survive; I could tell just from looking at it. Corners and edges poking through the cloth. All I could do was imagine what that sack contained.

Dangling from his back pocket hung a noisy chain attached to a large black leather wallet. The wallet, like Stiles, didn't try to hide its age but actually flaunted it. Brown spots and creases covered the package. The large silver chain protecting the wallet was the noisy alarm that said, "Stiles is coming." The pocketknife that hung from his belt signaled people, "I have strength."

His worn hiking boots looked as if they had seen much and traveled many places. A flannel blue and yellow plaid shirt covered a bright yellow polyester one hiding a few curly grey hairs that were trying to peek over the top. These two items completely clashed yet fit his personality. They also seemed to match his dusty grey pants with its small blue, yellow, green and red plaid.

We had an amazing conversation about his days working on a railroad and other life experiences. He was so interesting and had many things to say. He asked me what I was going to do with my life. I told him I had no idea. When he asked how old I was, I told him fifteen. He laughed and said I had lots of time to do whatever I wanted. This is when I asked about the button pinned to his jacket. "GO FLY A KITE," it read. He told me that he was a professional kite flyer and was on his way to a kite-flying convention in San Francisco.

He was one of the most interesting people I have ever met. He inspired me and helped me realize that I can do anything. Although I will probably never see him again, he had a big impact on me. I don't know what it was about him, but I will never forget him. 回

Photo by Vanessa Dawn Rand

Fallen Rock Zone

Fiction by Farrah Lehman

She's asleep, so I can't see her green eyes. Not that I want to see them. I mean, if they were in front of me, open and all, I wouldn't be repulsed by them. . . . Allie is asleep on my shoulder. Again. I try to move her so she'd lean her head against the window, so she could wake up and see the scenery flying past her outside the bus, instead of my neck and all the tired, drooling travelers around us. Allie is a poet, and everyone says that poets like scenery.

But she doesn't move. I think she knows what she's doing. She rests her head on my shoulder as though it's a sleepy accident, but she wants to be near me and she wants me to know what it's like to be near her. Or maybe it always is an accident. Maybe Allie's not as complicated as we all think.

No, that can't be true. She is unbelievably complicated—I don't think she can even figure herself out. I've read her poetry. I found her password-protected journal on her laptop computer when we were designing the Web site that got us on this bus in the first place. You can always get around passwords. I've read all the poems she never wanted me to read. Not necessarily never . . . I'm sure, in that strange little mind of hers, she imagined that

I'd find them someday. And she probably wrote a poem about that, too.

I can read Allie like a book, but that doesn't mean I understand her. I don't think she understands me either; she just likes to pretend she does. She finds some sort of great poetic romance in thinking that she knows everything there is to know about me. I wish she'd stick to bits and bytes here.

"Morning, Tom," she jokes, opening her eyes as the sun begins to set over the eight-hundredth fallen rock zone on the New York State Thruway. Her eyes are so green that they pierce through me. I wish they weren't so green. Then I wouldn't have to wonder what she's thinking.

"It's four-thirty in the afternoon, Lyric," I remind her. She finally lifts her head and smacks me on the arm.

"Don't call me that," she says. Allie pretends to hate her real name. But she doesn't, because all her poems are signed Lyric Allegra Sorenson. In fact, she entered the Web site design contest under that name. Lyric Allegra. Kind of interesting, if you think about it.

"Fallen Rock Zone," I read, looking past her. "Such a change in scenery." I roll my eyes. She loves sarcasm.

"There's another road sign," she says. *"Montreal—180 miles."*

"That's another three hours," I say. "You think any of those rocks ever fall?"

"What?"

"I mean, I wouldn't want a rock to fall down and crush you the day before our presentation."

"You're a moron, you know?" She pinches my cheek in

a very grandmotherly way. "It says *Fallen Rock Zone,* not falling rock zone. The rocks have already fallen."

"Thank you, Miss Young Grammarian."

"Oh . . . don't bother me. Remember that I corrected all your grammatical errors on the site." She finally lets go of my cheek.

It starts to get a bit awkward. All silence, no sarcasm. I wonder if I should tell her that Josie and I broke up last week. She knows. I'm sure Josie has already told her, and I'll bet that her heart is jumping, waiting for me to make the first move. Yeah, I know what you're thinking. Who does this guy think he is? Well, here's your answer—I don't know.

I think I might still want to be with Josie. She's safe and she's warm—but Allie chases after dreams and shadows and all these crazy things that can't be expressed in terms of bits and bytes or HTML code. I don't even completely know what she thinks of me. But Josie broke up with me because she said she didn't want to be tied down. Strange how Allie's sitting next to me, gazing out the window with her huge green eyes, and she's not tied down to anything.

We pull into a rest stop. "Twenty minutes, then the bus leaves," the driver announces.

Allie runs for the ladies' room. I buy us each a cup of coffee; I know she's going to reprimand me for buying her anything.

"Here you go, Lyric," I tell her, handing her the coffee when she's back to me. We're near the odd mixture of cement and nature that is the New York Thruway; it's a March sunset and it's so cold that our noses are running.

"Mmm . . . thanks, Tom." She takes a sip, then looks at me. "Okay, here we go. A—don't call me Lyric. B—don't ever buy anything for me again." She grins and, in the middle of a laugh, puts her free arm around my waist. I don't feel her arm, though; I only feel her pillowy coat. I put my free arm around her shoulders.

"All right, I get the point," I say.

She grins again. "It's now or never," she mutters.

"What?"

"Oh . . . did I just say that out loud?" Allie says. She's a real sneak . . . always pretending to be dizzy and misty and confused. "Hey . . . hey, Tom?"

"Yes?"

"I . . . I talked to Josie, you know. And . . . it's not . . . it doesn't have anything to do with . . . I . . . what would you think about us? Going out, you know? Just something we could . . . try for a while?"

"Yeah," I tell her. "I think we could try it for a while."

I keep my arm around her and I pull her a little closer. We walk back to the bus like two friends carrying the world between them. 回

Epilogue

by Melanie A. Rice

I t's in our songs, our words, our hearts. It makes life better, and sometimes worse. We'll often deny it or rush to embrace it. Love—it is our life. Love will stand by you in times of doubt and snatch you up sometimes by surprise. But love comes in many varieties, and it's certainly not a simple emotion. There's that unconditional, warm love your mother seems to overflow with, the kind that wraps around you and soothes the aches of loss and disappointment. Then there's *that* love—the kind that hits you like the bouncy ball of reality, smack in the face. You felt it every time you looked over in class and realized your crush was returning the glance! That feeling of complete contentment and peace, like an inexplicable high.

We have all felt love, and we all feel the need for it. It's vital to our spiritual survival, oxygen for our morale. It may be an obstacle in life to deal with—love and the turmoil it casually involves—but that love is the same goal we fight for. It is in every day, every person and every relationship. Someone once said, "Nothing lasts forever," and some relationships break up. That doesn't mean that you should never be willing to give your heart to another. You can't be afraid to open up and share all that you hold sacred. It may sound absurd, but you haven't lived until your heart's been broken.

Love is undeniably a part of us. It's what makes us human and humane. I used to think that it was cheesy when people said, "There's always someone who loves you." Funny how that changed. I realized that love can be subtle and sweet. It can be something as simple as a parent coming to your recital or asking how your day was, so innocently reassuring.

It truly does encompass all: our feelings, our thoughts, our lives—and this book. In this, the fourth in a monumental series, you have found hope, courage and voices. Voices of faith, experience—and love. It's that sharing of life that allows a book like this to emerge. Perhaps you have gained some perspective and hope for life. Love is there, it surrounds all of us, and this book is proof.

Melanie A. Rice, a high-school freshman, wrote the moving piece, "The Bus Ride," on page 226.

How to submit your writing, art and photos for the monthly *Teen Ink* magazine and the next *Teen Ink* book

You must be twelve to nineteen years old to be published.

- Include your name, year of birth, home address/ city/state/zip, telephone number and the name of your school (and English teacher) on each submission. For art and photos, place the information on the back of each piece. Please don't fold art.

- Type your submission, if possible, or print carefully in ink.

- We can't return any submissions, so keep a copy.

- Label all work fiction or nonfiction. Be sure to include a title.

- Please write this statement on each submission: "This will certify that the above work is completely original." Then sign your name.

- If you don't want your name published due to the very personal nature of a piece, we will respect your request, but you must include name and address information for our records.

Other Information

- If published in the magazine/book, you will receive a free copy together with an environmentally sound wooden pen and a special *Teen Ink* Post-it pad.

- All works submitted become the property of *Teen Ink* and all copyrights are assigned to *Teen Ink*. We retain the nonexclusive rights to publish all such works in any format. All material in *Teen Ink* is copyrighted to protect us and exclude others from republishing your work. However, all contributors retain the right to submit their work for publication elsewhere and you have our permission to do so.

- Writing may be edited; we reserve the right to publish our version without your approval.

Send submissions to:

Teen Ink
Box 97
Newton, MA 02461

On the Web: *www.TeenInk.com/Submissions*
By e-mail: *Book@TeenInk.com*

To learn more about the magazine and to request a free sample copy, see our Web site: *www.TeenInk.com*. Our phone number is 617-964-6800.

All the royalties from the *Teen Ink* books are donated to The Young Authors Foundation

Established in 1989, The Young Authors Foundation, Inc. is the publisher of *Teen Ink* (formerly *The 21st Century*), a monthly magazine written entirely by teens for teens. This magazine has been embraced by schools and teenagers nationwide with more than 3.5 million students reading it every year.

The magazine empowers teenagers by publishing their words, giving them a voice and demonstrating that they can make a difference. *Teen Ink* is dedicated to improving reading, writing and critical-thinking skills while encouraging creativity and building self-esteem. The editors have read more than 350,000 submissions from students during the past thirteen years, and more than 25,000 of them have been published. There is no charge to submit work and all published students receive a free copy of the magazine plus other items.

In keeping with its mission, the Foundation distributes thousands of class sets and individual copies free to schools and teachers every month. In addition, thousands of schools support the Foundation by paying a small fee for their monthly class sets.

From its beginnings as a small foundation with regional distribution of *Teen Ink,* The Young Authors Foundation has grown steadily and today is a national program funded through donations, sponsorships, grants and advertising from companies and individuals that support its goals. In addition to funding the magazine, the

Foundation underwrites a number of educational programs:

- *Teen Ink Poetry Journals* showcase more than one thousand young poets each year and are distributed free to subscribing schools.

- *Teen Ink Educator of the Year Awards Contest* welcomes nominating essays from students to honor outstanding teachers with cash prizes and publication of their essays in the magazine.

- *Teen Ink Book Awards* donates thousands of free books and award materials annually so schools can recognize students who have shown "improvement and individual growth in the field of English."

- *Teen Ink Interview Contest* encourages thousands of teens to interview family and friends with the winners interviewing national celebrities including Hillary Clinton, John Glenn, Maya Angelou, George Lucas, Jesse Jackson, R. L. Stine, Whoopi Goldberg and Michael Crichton.

- *Teen Ink Web site (www.TeenInk.com)* includes over 13,000 pages of student writing, art, photos, resources, contests and more.

The Young Authors Foundation, Inc. is a nonprofit 501(c)3 organization. See the next page for details on how you can become a member, support these programs and receive a monthly copy of the magazine.

Join The Young Authors Foundation and get a monthly subscription to *Teen Ink* magazine.

Foundation Supporters Receive:

- Ten months of *Teen Ink* magazine
- Annual Newsletter
- Partner in Education Satisfaction – You help thousands of teens succeed.

SUPPORT TEENS' VOICES!

The magazine includes stories, poems and art plus music, book and movie reviews, college essays, sports and more.

Only $25 per year

☐ **Annual Dues $25***
I want to receive ten monthly issues of *Teen Ink* magazine and become a supporter of The Young Authors Foundation.
(Enclose your check or complete credit card information below.)

☐ I am interested in your foundation. Please send me information about The Young Authors Foundation.

☐ I want to support the Foundation with a tax-deductible donation for $_____
(Do not send copies of the magazine.)

NAME_____PHONE_____

STREET_____

CITY/TOWN _____ STATE _____ ZIP _____

PHONE _____E-MAIL_____

M/C OR VISA *(CIRCLE ONE)*#_____ EXP. DATE ____/____

Send a gift subscription to:
NAME _____

STREET_____

CITY/TOWN_____STATE_____ZIP _____

Mail coupon to: Teen Ink • Box 97 • Newton, MA 02461 – Or join online: *www.TeenInk.com*

* The Young Authors Foundation, publisher of *Teen Ink*, is a 501(c)3 nonprofit organization providing opportunities for the education and enrichment of young people nationwide. While all donations support the Foundation's mission, 75% is designated for the magazine subscription, and no portion should be considered as a charitable contribution.

Acknowledgments

After thanking all the teenagers past and present who are responsible for making this book possible, we must also give our heartfelt thanks to all those who have done so much to make the *Teen Ink* book series a reality. When we started publishing *Teen Ink* magazine in the late 1980s, we never imagined that we would be working with so many talented and devoted people. Some have played an enormous role in the overall success of our nonprofit Young Authors Foundation (that helps fund all our projects). Others devote themselves tirelessly to our monthly magazine that is the source for the *Teen Ink* books. Many more gave their time, skills and insight, and we are most fortunate to have all of these people in our lives:

Our Children:

Robert Meyer, Alison Meyer Hong, and her husband, Michael, have been a never-ending source of support from the very beginning, when they were teenagers themselves. Their love, encouragement and wisdom continue to guide us every step of the way.

Our Staff:

We couldn't have done it without our *other* family: our magazine staff filled with young, helpful voices who are always there with words to advise and assist: Kate Dunlop Seamans, Karen Watts, Tony Abeln, Lindsay Mekemson, Denise Peck, and our longtime volunteer, Barbara Field, who has been a support through the years, and the college and high-school interns who've been a tremendous help in many ways. In addition we appreciate the efforts of our extended staff, which includes Cathi Dunn MacRae who again helped with the reading and evaluation of pieces, Paul Watts, Larry Reed, Glenn Koenig and the folks at Saltus Press.

Our Family, Friends and Foundation Board:

We always depend on our extended family and friends who are there for us on many levels: Relatives: The Raisners (Barbara, Debra, Jason, David, Amy and Amber), Joseph Rice III, Jennifer and Rick Geisman, Audrey, Jennifer and Lindsay Powers, Susan Costello and her gang, the Abel family, the Hongs, Alison Swap and Tyler, Willie and Eubie. Friends: Barbara Wand, Mollie and Steve Dunn, Timothy Neeley, Filis Casey, Paul Chase, Paula and Lowell Fox, Stewart and Jackie Newland. And the Foundation Board Members: J. Robert Casey, David Anable, Richard Freedberg, and our Advisory Board: Beverly Beckham, Michael Dukakis, Milton Lieberman, Harold Raynolds, Susan Weld and Thomas Winship who have served with us through the years.

Our Publishing Family at HCI:

We, of course, once again thank all the folks at HCI who have published, promoted and believed in our project: Peter Vegso, the number-one man; Tom Sand, Lisa Drucker, Susan Tobias, Terry Burke, Lori Golden,

Irena Xanthos, Kim Weiss, Paola Fernandez, Kelly Maragni, and special thanks to Larissa Hise Henoch and her staff for their continued design creativity and support. In addition, we want to thank the following incredible teachers and their more than four thousand students who managed to read and evaluate sample chapters for *Teen Ink: Love and Relationships* during a time of great stress for our country. Their feedback and ratings were invaluable in helping us to select the final pieces for this book.

Attleboro High School, Attleboro, Massachusetts—Adeline Bee
Auburn High School, Auburn, New York—Preston Wilson
Bay Port High School, Bay Port, Wisconsin—Michael Roherty
Bellport High School, Brookhaven, New York—Glenn Hadzima
Bristol Eastern High School, Bristol, Connecticut—Dorothy Ammerman
Central Bucks East High School, Doylestown, Pennsylvania—Marie Kane
Colonial Forge High School, Stafford, Virginia—Lisa Renard
Concord High School, Elkhart, Indiana—Chris Judson
Cortez High School, Phoenix, Arizona—Tom Helms and Diane Bykowski
Dobson High School, Mesa, Arizona—Susan Brenden and E. A. Viator
Druid Hills High School, Atlanta, Georgia—Sherrie Crow
East Middle High School, Butte, Montana—Donna Jean Pickett
El Dorado High School, El Dorado, Kansas—Heather Luginbill
Exeter Area High School, Exeter, New Hampshire—John Ferguson
Fitch Senior High School, Groton, Connecticut—Jeri DeSantis
Frontier Central High School, Hamburg, New York—Tom Roberts
Garfield Middle School, Revere, Massachusetts—Lisa Spinelli
Glenbard East High School, Lombard, Illinois—Bill Littell
Griswold High School, Griswold, Connecticut—Nadine Keane
Hillsboro-Deering High School, Hillsboro, New Hampshire—Beffa Ommaya Wyldemoon
Iola-Scandinavia School, Iola, Wisconsin—Mary McClone
Kamehameha Secondary School, Honolulu, Hawaii—Ruth Canham
Liberty High School, Liberty, South Carolina—Lori Gwinn

Marshfield Junior High School, Marshfield, Wisconsin—Richard Halle

Mercy High School, Middletown, Connecticut—Adrienne Lovell and Leslie Chausse

Mount Saint Charles Academy, Woonsocket, Rhode Island—Donald Hogue

Murray High School, Murray, Utah—Crystal Spackman

Papillion LaVista High School, Papillion, Nebraska—Margaret Shanahan

Patrick Henry High School, Ashland, Virginia—Sallie Bedall

Pine-Richland Middle School, Gibsonia, Pennsylvania—Susan Frantz, Aleta Lardin, John Dolphin, Janet Hanlon and Kathy Mervin

Poudre High School, Fort Collins, Colorado—Kathryn Symmes

Randolph High School, Randolph, New Jersey—Elizabeth McConnell

Rippowam Cisqua School, Bedford, New York—Cathy Greenwood

Sebring McKinley High School, Sebring, Ohio—Nicole Herman

Shoreham-Wading River High School, Shoreham, New York—Kevin Mann

St. Albans High School, St. Albans, West Virginia—Bettijane Burger

Stamford High School, Stamford, Connecticut—Diane Drugge

Stratford High School, Goose Creek, South Carolina—Susan Halloran

Suffern High School, Suffern, New York—Greg Casarella

Washington Junior High School, Toledo, Ohio—Lori Bosch

Watertown High School, Watertown, Tennessee—Lynda Jellison

Williamsville South High School, Williamsville, New York—Lisabeth Pieters

Winnisquam Regional High School, Tilton, New Hampshire—Barbara Blinn

Contributors

Rachel Anderson is a freshman in college majoring in visual arts and communications. In high school, she kept herself busy serving as president of the Art Club, treasurer of the Student Government, and a member of the Student Advisory Council to her state's Board of Education. Rachel's poignant piece was originally published in *Teen Ink* magazine during her senior year. She would like to thank her family for making her life as wonderful as possible, and sends a special thank-you out to her mom for doing such a good job.

Denise Ankel moved to the United States from Germany this year, entering high school as a sophomore. She says her favorite memory is her first day at an American high school when she met many new people and saw what they were like. She loves to play the drums and hang out, doing nothing in particular with her friends. This is the first photograph Denise has ever had published—she didn't know a thing about photography until she came here. She would like to thank her friend at school who encouraged her to take her first photo class.

Liz Antle is a freshman in college majoring in English, though her moving story about a renegade friend first appeared in *Teen Ink* magazine when she was a senior in high school. In addition to her English skills, Liz is also known for her wacky adventures in baby-sitting. A recent experience involved an unexpected birthday party and a broken dining-room table, but luckily Liz handled the situation with grace and ease. When not fending off baby-sitting disasters, Liz can be found writing or painting, her two favorite things. She would like to thank her mother for always supporting her writing.

Jeff Antonucci is a junior in high school where he enjoys taking photographs. This interesting silhouette of two friends was snapped as a moment that expressed emotion. Jeff loves sailing, snowboarding, hiking and just plain staying active, although he's not a team player. He's also into music, including reggae, classic rock and especially Bob Marley!

Lauren Sue Asperschlager wrote her piece about her quirky music teacher as a junior in high school, where she was a National Merit Scholar Finalist. Now a senior in college, Lauren still enjoys playing the trumpet in several musical ensembles. In addition, she is an active member of her church and the Salvation Army. Lauren emphasizes that "every day of my life is a wonderful gift from God that must never be taken for granted."

Daniel Bailey enjoys playing the piano and the guitar, reading, and just about any athletic activity, especially football. His poem was originally published in *Teen Ink* magazine at the end of his high-school career, and now Daniel is a sophomore in college double majoring in secondary education/physics and English. He hopes to be a teacher or a principal one day, as well as a writer. Daniel is currently working on his first children's book.

Patrick Michael Baird took his photo as a senior in high school using a Canon Rebel G. Now a college sophomore studying photography and psychology, most of his time and energy go into his school projects and photography. In his spare time he likes to visit galleries and museums and enjoy the city nightlife. Patrick thanks his former photography teacher, Ms. Demetrious, for being a huge inspiration, as well as his friends and family for their support, guidance and love.

Alexis Bargelski lived with her family in Seoul, Korea for six years. During that time, she traveled all over Asia and knows that her experience abroad will always have a huge impact on her life. While she wrote her piece about her adopted sister as a senior in high school, Alexis is now in college pursuing a degree in business administration. She would like to thank her sister Tessa, her parents and Mrs. Lowell for encouraging her to submit her story for publication.

Marc R. Baron graduated from college with a degree in political science and a minor in English. He loves poetry and progressive politics and has a charming four-year-old son who is the love his life. Marc saw this portrait of a very special day with his dad published in *Teen Ink* magazine when he was a junior in high school.

Alexandra Berger is loving her sophomore year in college. She's meeting wonderful, colorful people, taking classes and trying to travel as much as possible. She hasn't gotten too involved on campus yet, aside from the music scene, but she's working on it. Her moving piece originally ran in *Teen Ink* magazine when she was a sophomore in high school. Alexandra would like to send a thank-you out "to anybody who's changed my mind."

Sierra Black is now a professional freelance writer, but she'll never forget seeing her work in print for the first time in *Teen Ink* magazine when she was seventeen years old. She has won several awards and received recognition for her short stories and poems. She graduated from college as a writing major, and is currently working toward her M.F.A. Besides the written word, Sierra has three other loves: travel and her two cats.

Kelli Bollin took her close-up of this woodpile in her backyard as part of her photography class last year. Sending it to *Teen Ink* magazine was part of her final exam, where she saw it published. Now in high school, she plans to continue her interest in photography, but is currently focusing her artistic energies on oil pastel and drawing. She particularly enjoys capturing people in her artwork.

Kristen Bonacorso took her photo as a junior in high school. Now in her third year of college, she enjoys hanging out with her friends and "could spend hours looking at photographs." She is a big fan of Ansel Adams and especially appreciates black-and-white photography and the use of contrasting textures. After eating only grilled cheese and French toast for seven years, Kristen has learned to love food and appreciate it as an art itself. She also loves the beach and going for drives to enjoy the ocean scenery.

Sara Booth took her shot of the two pensive teens after a long night at the prom and gave each a print as a remembrance. She now works in an art gallery for children and has even had her own photography show of photos taken when she visited Spain. She loves art, writing, reading and skiing!

Julie Nicole Boucher wrote her piece when she was still in high school dealing with a recent move from her childhood home. She has since graduated from college, initially wanting to be a journalist. She was so inspired by those who helped her grandfather during his struggle trying to communicate after a stroke, she has been studying for her masters in speech pathology. Julie would like to dedicate her piece to Maryanne Marmi, a special teacher who showed her the power of the written word, and to her parents, who showed her the resiliency of the human heart, and unconditional love and support.

Hadley Breed had many of her photographs published in *Teen Ink* magazine during her high-school career. These two decorated females appeared earlier this year. In addition to photography, Hads swims and plays lacrosse for her high school and is a ski instructor! She would like to thank her photography teacher, for without him she wouldn't be in this book!

Danielle Brown adores all kinds of photography and took this shot of her two sisters recently. A senior, she plans to continue her study of photography in college, especially enjoying the work of photojournalist Dorothea Lange. Danielle, who works after school, also likes to write and plays the violin in her high-school orchestra.

Matt Bullock is just finishing middle school where he shot this interesting perspective of a highway through a fence and actually entered it in a contest! He likes photography and thinks he will continue it in high school. He really enjoys skating and playing baseball. Matt's photo appeared in *Teen Ink* magazine last fall.

Liz Cashman is a crazy, fun person who loves to take pictures. A sophomore in college, she shot this pensive picture in high school and wants to thank Jeffie for being such a cutie-pie and therefore enabling her to take wonderful photographs!

Ena Chang wrote this fictionalized piece about asking that guy to the prom back when she was still in high school. She has since graduated from college and now lives with her shar-pei, Simon.

Jenn Christian has been published a number of times in *Teen Ink* magazine. She loves shooting photographs and was experimenting with different light sources when she shot this photo of her sister using a strobe light in a dark room. Jenn is also very active in sports, playing softball and field hockey as a junior in high school. She also is quite involved with her school's Model UN and hopes to go into politics.

Katherine Cincotta wrote her poignant poem as a senior in high school. In addition to writing, she enjoyed playing soccer and pitching for her school's varsity softball team. She loves art and takes classes in drawing and painting outside of school. She is now in college and hopes to pursue teaching or writing.

Martha Collins loves to write, and she is also very involved in her community. She works at a local animal clinic and hopes to become a veterinarian someday. She's also a cheerleader and the winner of her local beauty/talent pageant. Martha, now a sophomore, wrote the story of her adoption last year. She would like to thank her parents for bringing her into their lives and standing by her through all the rough times they have shared.

Brooke Cooper, originally from England, is one of six children. Her favorite memories range from desperately wanting to be Tina Turner at age three to backpacking through Europe later in life. In her spare time, she enjoys rifle shooting at clay pigeons. Brooke's nostalgic poem about friendship was first published in *Teen Ink* magazine when she was a junior in high school. Now in college majoring in education and minoring in religion, she hopes one day to go on a mission to Russia to teach.

Emily J. Copeman began writing her own column in her town's newspaper when she was eleven. She continues to love to write and read and hopes to pursue a career in journalism. She is graduating from high school this year where she has been active in drama and loves working for the fine-arts department. Last year, shortly after "Jack" was published in *Teen Ink* magazine, she and Jack decided to take a break, but are still very close friends, talking almost every day. Emily believes they will remain a part of each other's lives forever.

Lea Ann Coreau remembers a big winter storm during her junior year in high school when she was inspired to shoot her photo using her Minolta 400SI camera. Now a college sophomore studying graphic arts and photography, she is a member of ASPCA and the Humane Society. In her free time she enjoys hanging out with her family's dog and three cats, as well as her friends. Her dream job is to take pictures for *National Geographic* or *Rolling Stone* one day. Lea Ann thanks her high-school photography teachers, Ed Warner and Joseph DeRuvo, Jr., and her best friends and fellow photographers, Pam Torok (whose photo appears in this book) and Sarah Christensen.

Nicole C. Corvey recently wrote this poignant poem about her grand-father. A sophomore in high school, she is active in many clubs and will soon be on the track team. She volunteers at a local humane society where she loves to play with all the puppies and kittens. She has always wanted to write something to her grandfather and dedicates the poem to him.

Lindsey E. Cronin was into lots of activities in high school: soccer, golf, student council, orchestra and work, as evidenced by her moving piece published in *Teen Ink* magazine when she was a senior. Loving her first year at college, she plans to double major in English and litera-ture and keeps busy with intramural lacrosse, orchestra (to give her that necessary music fix) and a service organization where she is putting together a project to support divorced parents in helping their children adjust. Lindsay would love to dedicate her piece to Norman.

Susan DeBiasio has fond memories of being published back in high school when she was a prolific writer. Published in *Teen Ink* magazine when she was a senior, "To Be Old Like Uma" depicts the reality that older folks are actually freed of many of the daily stresses and reduced to the simplistic perceptions of children. Her other poem, "Gram," describes her precious grandmother. Unfortunately she finds little time to write now since she is a full-time Web designer, which she loves, although she has a long commute to work. She does enjoy painting, and has four ferrets for roommates: Cathy, Ralph, Daisy and Alice.

Laura Dickinson writes all the time—she thinks it's a great outlet for her emotions. She maintains a Web site featuring her work that she updates daily. Her poem originally appeared in *Teen Ink* magazine when she was a senior in high school. Now Laura is in college majoring in English and minoring in music and drama. She dedicates her poem to her high-school teachers: "You have been my support for so long, and you are still behind me, and that fact gives me constant strength."

Dan Durbin is currently a senior in high school. His poignant piece about fitting in was published in *Teen Ink* magazine just this past fall. In addition to writing, he enjoys playing many sports including football, baseball and tennis. Dan is also really into music and loves to sing and play the guitar in his spare time. Dan would like to thank Mrs. Pearson for encouraging him to write and all his friends and family for supporting him in everything he does.

Susan A. Eldred wrote her piece about her interracial relationship as a senior in high school where she was also the senior editor of her school newspaper. Loving college, Susan is majoring in anthropology and minoring in English and art. In her free time, she is busy singing with her band, Honey Bee, and working with a professor on a Web site that deals with regional religious centers.

Melissa Robin Fadul's most memorable experience was playing on an all-woman's baseball team for two years. During a more recent trip to Arizona, Melissa discovered her new favorite state. She wrote her piece during her senior year of high school, and she would like to thank her parents for their support, her brother for keeping her laughing, her girlfriend for being "the most beautiful person I've ever met and giving me the confidence to cross every path I need to," and her friend Julie just for being Julie.

Nicole Flannery penned this moving poem as a senior in high school when it appeared in *Teen Ink* magazine. Involved in drama and the yearbook, Nicole was also a peer helper. After high school, she joined the Army for a four-year stint, traveling to Korea and the Middle East. She now works for a telecommunications company and recently had a son. She and Alexander's father love to go to sporting events, museums and theater.

Kenneth L. Flewelling has kept the creative juices flowing since his poem was originally published in *Teen Ink* magazine during his senior year of high school. Graduating from college with a major in media arts, he went on to work in TV and theater while making independent documentaries on the side. You may even have seen some of his work: His American Red Cross fiftieth anniversary spot ran during last year's Super Bowl. Right now, he is working on a documentary about rural Maine communities.

J. A. Gaeta, or Jeff to his friends, will graduate from college this year with a degree in civil engineering. He extends a special thank-you to Melikka and Paul Perron, Julie Gaeta, and Kerri-Anne Logan: "I love you very much."

Amybeth Gardner loves the music of Elton John and was recently able to show him her appreciation by giving him flowers at a concert. When she's not interacting with celebrities, she may be found taking a writing workshop or working on a research team, perhaps looking into the eating patterns of various college populations. Amybeth also loves to run, especially in the rain. Her pieces, the poignant portrait of her beloved teacher and amazing connection to Carly Simon, were originally published in *Teen Ink* magazine during her senior year of high school.

Alex Golub-Sass is finishing his junior year of high school, and recently took this shot of his older sister and her boyfriend. He enjoys shooting landscapes and credits Ansel Adams as his inspiration. He is a lacrosse player, and also participates in the math team at his school.

Jessica Gonzalez is an active freshman in college who enjoys doing ballet, running, Rollerblading and shopping. She is majoring in broadcast journalism and one day hopes to be a television news anchor. Jessica works at a coffee shop, which explains why she is addicted to caffeine, and on weekends she keeps the animals happy at the Humane Society. She loves the Charles Swindoll quote, which she tries to live by: "Life is 10 percent what happens to you and 90 percent how you react to it." Her piece was originally published in *Teen Ink* magazine when she was a high-school senior.

Noah Gordon is an avid social activist and musician. He is in two bands—one that plays experimental folk and the other with a punk/ska edge—and publishes a magazine devoted to encouraging tolerance and unity between races, genders, social classes and sexual identities. His atmospheric work about chess in Washington Square first appeared in *Teen Ink* magazine when Noah was a sophomore in high school.

Jamie Graham loves observing: people, animals, nature. This is the root of her inspiration to write. She is sure she will be a park bench in her next life. She recently wrote her stirring piece about her father. Although she is still struggling to connect with him, she has hopes that things will improve. A senior in high school, Jamie wants to send thanks to a very special teacher, Gail, for her constant support and advice.

Amanda R. Grier loves to travel and meet people with different perspectives. She recently returned from a college semester in Japan, and after she graduates this year, will be packing her bags for a year or two of public service abroad. Amanda's insightful piece was published in *Teen Ink* magazine during her senior year of high school. She says, "I never give enough thanks for my best friend and role model, Jesus Christ. Thank you for never giving up on me and always showing me amazing discoveries about the world. Also, thanks to Scott who every day is more like Christ."

Christopher Gubelmann loves the outdoors—give him a trail to hike, a pole to fish with, a tent to camp in, or a dirt bike to ride and he's one happy high-school senior. He also enjoys leading his church youth group and playing lacrosse for his school. Chris hopes to use his love of drawing in a future career as a graphic designer for clothing or possibly as an architect. He thanks God, his parents, Rebels Six and the Highlands Crew, Mr. Kavanah and his school, and anyone who has appreciated his work and encouraged him to write.

Nicole M. Gulla is a sophomore in college where she is majoring in art and computer science. She took this arresting photo of a young girl in braces as a senior in high school when it was published in *Teen Ink* magazine.

Ryan Healy enjoys playing basketball and softball as a junior in high school. Living near the seashore, this photo was a natural subject for Ryan who takes photography classes in school. During vacations he loves traveling to California and Maine. He'd like to dedicate his shot to his photography teacher, who taught him all he knows!

Mallory Ho, or "Mal" to her buddies, loves to dance. Now in her senior year of high school, she has been on the drill/flag/dance team since freshman year, and this is her second year as team captain. If she's not dancing, look for her at the YMCA with her all-girls service/social club, probably sipping green tea and having ice cream, which she says she can eat almost any time of the day. Mal thanks her sophomore English teacher, Robin, for encouraging her to submit her lovely poem about friendship to *Teen Ink* magazine.

Destie Hohman worked her way through college doing everything from waiting tables to tutoring inner-city kids and being a lab technician for a pottery lab. She majored in international politics and pottery—quite a combo! She just passed her physical on her way to being an intelligence officer in the Marine Corps. In high school, when her amusing portrait of her mother's cooking was published in *Teen Ink* magazine, she was into everything. She said it's amazing she found time to write with her involvement in band, drama, dance, chorus and student government, as well as working. She likes being busy!

Anna Isaacson dedicates her story to Rose Vago Magyar, her great-grandmother. She is currently a sophomore in high school and loves music and sports. She sings, plays the piano, the flute and the guitar, and enjoys skiing, field hockey and lacrosse. Right now, she wants to be a doctor or a teacher, but, regardless of her career, she hopes to do something interesting and useful during her life.

Ed Jaffe has had many of his photographs published in *Teen Ink* magazine during the last few years. This shot of a busy intersection was taken when he was testing out how slowing his shutter speed would blur one of the cars. He works for a commercial photographer, although he's not sure if this will be his life's work. He plays the tenor sax in the jazz band, and loves to act and direct. He also skis and is a lifeguard. He's one busy person!

Adam Janko graduated from high school a few years ago and works as a manager for a sporting-goods store as well as helping coach the high-school wrestling team. He continues to enjoy photography, taking his close-up of these musical instruments in high school. Engaged to be married, he loves to cook and bike in his spare time.

Dyani Jensen's photo of four smiling teens was originally published in *Teen Ink* magazine when she was a senior in high school. These days she is studying industrial engineering. In her spare time, Dyani enjoys stamping, scrapbooking and reading. She is something of a people person, too: She loves to spend time with her two children and to meet new people.

Lisa Kelly is on the Academic Decathlon Team, works on her school newspaper, and plays softball and soccer. She enjoys skiing and water-skiing with her friends and family. A senior in high school, Lisa is active in her church and is a CCD assistant. She would like to thank her family and her "eleven" for all their help and support. She would like to dedicate her funny, insightful story to Kate F. and in memory of Don Juan.

Lena Koroleva is a sophomore in high school. She is a member of the Model UN and has been involved with the crew for school musical performances. In her free time she enjoys photography, playing piano and tennis, traveling and meeting people. (She just returned from a two-week trip to Paris!) She also loves to dance and recently started taking hip-hop dance classes. Lena's photo appeared in *Teen Ink* magazine last year. To her parents she says, "Thank you, and I love you."

Michele Kulis was in her junior-year Spanish class when she realized she had forgotten to bring her completed roll of film for a photography assignment that was due the following period. She quickly shot another roll of film using her fellow classmates as models (thanks to her Spanish teacher who was "a great sport"). Michele is now attending college and studying her other love: computer science. In her free time she enjoys going to the movies and taking lots of pictures of her daughter, Sarah.

Erik DeRosa Lattimore finally did get his license after several tries! His hilarious piece was published in *Teen Ink* magazine a couple of years ago when he was a sophomore in high school. He really loves to ski and is currently editor of his school yearbook, which entails a lot of responsibility. He has a real talent for the computer, troubleshooting to earn a few dollars, and he plans to pursue computer science in college.

Jesse Legon started taking photography when he was in high school and discovered he really liked it, taking pictures at sporting events. He loves action photography and always tries to capture the moment. He took this chess player in Washington Square Park in Manhattan while he was observing the players. He is a huge sports fan and plays soccer and tennis.

Farrah Lehman wrote her piece while still in high school, the first of many short stories she wrote. Farrah, majoring in creative writing, saw one of her plays take life on stage in a major production. While still in college she finished her first book of short stories, *Blueberry Bridesmaids,* which was published last July. She wishes to thank her high-school English teacher.

Jasmin Lehmann is Swiss and was staying with an American host family last year when she shot this tree in the snow just before sunset on a clear winter day. Jasmin said, "There was a very special atmosphere, and I wanted to catch it with my camera." She loved photography from the first moment she started and would like to thank her photography teacher, Mrs. Lowe, and her host family who is her second family now.

Margot Leifer wrote about this difficult relationship with her friend as a senior in high school. Into a number of clubs, her real love was theater, especially musicals. Margot performed in a number of shows in high school as well as doing some community theater productions of Neil Simon plays. Now a junior in college, she has settled on studying accounting, realizing that theater wasn't a practical career. She is active in her sorority where she is philanthropy chair, and still does some writing.

Chelsea Lettieri, now a college freshman, has loved to write ever since she was little. This particular poem, an insightful tale about a car ride with her crush, was published in *Teen Ink* magazine when she was a sophomore in high school. Chelsea also enjoys playing softball and swimming, and she always makes time to spend with her family and friends.

Jason Li is graduating from high school this year and plans to study computer science in college. His heartfelt piece about his uncle appeared in *Teen Ink* magazine last year. Jason, very active in his church, especially enjoys playing basketball there and says that even though he is quite short, he makes up for his height with his speed. He would very much like to return to Fujhen where his uncle still lives.

Kendra Lider-Johnson began her first novel in fourth grade and never stopped writing. Another piece by Kendra, "The Longest Hallway," appeared in *Teen Ink 2: More Voices, More Visions.* She was deeply involved in both her high school and college literary magazines, and turned her love for words to her new career in the publishing industry.

She found a new perspective on writing and literature through Toni Morrison's *The Bluest Eye* and Virginia Woolf's *To the Lighthouse*.

Esther Ling spent this past year studying in Japan as part of her senior year of high school. Her major interests include music and sports. She enjoys playing the guitar and piano, but singing has been a part of her life for as long as she can remember. She has played basketball since her brother taught her in elementary school. In Japan, Esther also joined the Kyudo Club, which is traditional Japanese archery. She is very interested in Asian languages and culture, and wants to study Japanese, Mandarin, Korean, International Business and English writing in college. Published in *Teen Ink* magazine a couple of years ago, she dedicates her short story to her mom who has shown her the joy that can come from putting words on paper.

Linda Liu has always been an avid reader and writer, working on her college newspaper as arts editor, critiquing films. Now she's decided to pursue her Ph.D. so she can become an English professor. In high school she was just beginning to discover contemporary poetry, helping her formulate these two insightful gems that appeared in *Teen Ink* magazine. She also had a zeal for track and field as well as cross-country. She's always been interested in writing, even though she hasn't written poetry lately, and recently has been focused on creative non-fiction and criticism.

Amanda J. Luzar took this photograph during her junior year of high school. She recently graduated and begins college in the fall. Amanda was born in Germany and lived in Singapore for some time before moving to the United States three years ago. She would like to thank her model in the photo, Lisa, and her dog, Gypsie.

Alex Marquez took this shot of a pensive young woman a few years ago when he was in high school. He just completed college where he became licensed to be a marine technician. He loves football and was captain of his team that went to the Super Bowl and was undefeated! He was selected as best defensive player and an all-star. He was also a wrestler, coming in fifth in the state.

Sandy Medeiros has continued her interest in photographing, majoring in film/video and animation in college. Her interesting shot was published in *Teen Ink* magazine when she was a senior in high school.

Yaniris Mejia, called Lily by her friends, recently enjoyed several exciting changes in her life—she began her first year of college, moved to a new state and got married! At college she is pursuing a degree in communications. Her heartwarming photo of a couple on a swing was originally published in *Teen Ink* magazine when she was a senior in high school. Lily thanks the Boston Photo Collaborative for three years of wonderful photography experience, and she thanks *Teen Ink* for sharing her work with others.

Shannon P. Miller, after receiving a degree in elementary education and teaching for a year, decided that teaching wasn't for her after all. She took some time off and discovered a love for the newspaper world! She now does layout and production for a small newspaper and has a chance to write, which she really enjoys. Her realistic short story was published by *Teen Ink* magazine when she was a senior in high school after she had a dream about this "guy" who was actually a hockey player for the Bruins whom she had always "admired from afar."

Summer A. Miller took this photo with her very first roll of film as a sophomore in high school where her love for photography began. This shot was trying something with a bit of depth and perhaps a romantic feel to it using an old Pentax K100, which she still cherishes. After high school, she studied photography in Paris for a while and still shoots a roll now and then. But interior design is her new love, although she's definitely interested in film. She credits her amazing photography teacher, Greg Storm: "He allowed me the freedom with my photographic endeavors that I really needed. Thanks, Strommy!" And thanks to everyone who supported her photographic endeavors: her family, the Cushmans and, especially, Ian.

Rachel Mitchem takes after her mother in that she loves to act and dance. Someday she hopes to make a career of these talents. In any case, she can use her dancing skills to follow in her mother's footsteps that Rachel describes in her day-in-the-life tale. Rachel says that she would like to thank her mother and brother for giving her so much fun and excitement in the early morning hours, and for providing so much to write about.

Shari Moore wrote her tender portrait of her brother while still a sophomore in high school. Shari keeps very busy with school activities (student government, marching band and ski club, to name a few) and is looking forward to studying pre-law in college as she prepares for a career in corporate law. Even though she juggles her schoolwork, many extracurriculars and a job, she loves to spend time with all of her best friends and thanks them for making her sixteenth birthday great.

Mark J. Murphy, now a high-school junior, is a young romantic who loves to love. He says Katelyn, the girl in his story, still holds a piece of his heart even though they have grown apart. His new girlfriend, Kristen, is his "earth angel" and he loves everything about her. Mark also enjoys adventure and the finer things in life. If he had to describe himself he would say he is "passionate" and "idealistic." Mark believes that "the time we have on Earth should be enjoyed, every moment should be taken advantage of. I try to make every day better than yesterday and the next day even better." He dedicates his piece to everyone who has supported him in following his dreams, and to a very special woman, Mrs. Marie Kane, for all her love and guidance.

Beth Anne Nadeau wrote her nostalgic poem during her senior year in high school. She has since graduated from college where she studied creative writing and rhetoric and was a member of the National English Honor Society. A few years ago, her mother was in a car accident that left her in a coma for fifteen days. For her senior thesis, Beth and her mother collaborated on a book recounting her mother's experiences while comatose and through her recovery.

Emily Newick recently graduated from college where she majored in Latin American studies and minored in geography. Emily wrote this insightful portrait of her grandmother a number of years ago and it was published in *Teen Ink* magazine when she was a junior in high school. She dedicates it to her grandmother who is still living today at the age of ninety-one.

George L. Newton III, published in *Teen Ink* magazine his senior year of high school, says that every day his heart grows stronger with the love he gives and receives. Now a college senior pursuing an English major, he still writes in every spare second, trying to trap his thoughts on paper before they disappear. He admits that he is scared but hopeful of his chances to make the world a better place. George would like to remind us that "Love is the greatest gift you can give."

Scott Nichols succeeded, despite the abuse that he movingly depicts in his poem, written while a senior in high school. Now a college junior majoring in business, Scott plans to go to law school and study sports and entertainment law. He is an avid sports fan (especially of basketball), and loves children. He is also a college representative for a major music company.

Astride Noel started taking photographs just last year, but she loves it. She is also into theater, mock trial and works part-time. A busy junior, Astride also loves to write, especially poetry. One of her poems appeared in *Teen Ink* magazine this past year. This photo was taken of her sister and her little girl when Astride asked them to "hug."

Shana Onigman graduated from college with a degree in theater and music. She enjoys road biking, swimming, hiking, playing the violin and participating in theater. She recently decided that she would like to study to become a cantor. Shana was published many times in high school and wrote her essay during her senior year. She described the first time she was published in *Teen Ink* magazine with a line from a James Taylor song: "The sky opened and the earth shook."

Cynthia Oquendo, so eloquent in her story about a long-lost friend, says that sometimes she is so quiet she can't hear herself. Writing, acting in school musicals and dancing alone in her room are her expressive answers to the subdued characteristics that earned her the nickname "Stoneface." A senior in high school, Cynthia is getting in touch with her Puerto Rican heritage by "trying desperately to pin down the Spanish language," and she plans to cultivate her creative side as a writer/artist/actress, moonlighting as a waitress. She dedicates her story to Mr. Cherry.

Urszula Paliwoda is now studying graphic design, physiology and neurobiology in college where she is incredibly busy planning homecoming and major concerts. She traveled back to Poland, her homeland, with her mother and brother last summer, and teaches Web design to young people. Her depiction of Ann was published in *Teen Ink* magazine when she was a junior in high school.

Sara Elise Panzner recalls that she and her friends were just "having fun and trying different things" when she took her photo as a senior in high school. Now a college sophomore studying communications and sociology, she hopes to work in the fashion industry some day. In her free time she enjoys dancing, shopping and hanging out with her friends. She also loves to travel, especially "anywhere warm and populated." Sara thanks her photography teacher and her friends who had so much fun posing for her.

Lynda Park loves to play piano and relaxes by taking long walks in cool weather. She once taught a third-grade class in an inner-city school in high school, which inspired her to want to teach once she graduates from college. Her piece appeared in *Teen Ink* magazine when she was a sophomore in high school, and she thanks her mom, dad, Unni, and her grandma.

Lindsay R. Pattison is graduating from high school this year and is determined to become a surgeon, her dream for years. She volunteers at a hospital and frequently shadows an anesthesiologist. Her brave piece, published last year, verbalized for her a challenging stage most teens experience. She's glad she's gained strength from it and applied it to other tough decisions she's faced. She is active in her church and was in charge of a mentoring program for middle-school girls called, appropriately, Girl2Girl.

David Pease keeps himself very busy with high school (he's number two in his class), student council and sports (primarily track and soccer). David wants to graduate from college and then explore the world, although he knows he'll probably have different dreams every few weeks. He shared the room in his poem with his brother Ben, whom he would like to thank for inspiring him.

Adrienne A. Perry remembers how wonderful she felt when her moving story of facing tragedy was first published in *Teen Ink* magazine. She has gone on to become a technical writer at a software-development firm. In the little free time she has, she likes to read and hike with her pet poodle, Noodle. Adrienne thanks her "partner in crime," Jessy, for keeping her interested in writing, and dedicates her work to her fiancé (her high-school sweetheart) who inspired her writing.

Jenny Pirkle likes working with language—now in college, she is working toward an English major with an emphasis in writing and a minor in French. In high school, she served as the French club secretary, and this slice-of-life was published in *Teen Ink* magazine when she was a senior. Jenny also enjoys acting, and has performed in or done technical work for every play performed during her high-school career. She continues to work backstage for her college's theater. Though she never knew his name and never saw him again, Jenny dedicates this piece to the subject of her story, the "strange-looking boy."

Dwayne J. Price wrote his loving portrait of his aunt, Anna Louise Maurer, last year, as a sophomore in high school. He has a passion for music, playing flute in his high-school band and singing both in choir and in a Christian rock band called "Lost No More." DJ is also a camp counselor and is very active in his church. He thanks God for all the talents bestowed on him.

Beth Bednarz Pruski originally wrote her piece about her mother as a senior in high school. Beth is now married and has a two-year-old daughter. She began her professional career as a volunteer staff nurse at a medical shelter for the homeless and currently works as a nurse specializing in cardiac surgery. Although her story reflects some of the more difficult aspects of their relationship, Beth is now full of love, admiration and appreciation for her mom.

Beth M. Putnam skis, plays tennis, reads, and enjoys spending time with her family and friends. She's also an explorer who loves to meet new people and visit new places. She wrote her poem as a freshman in high school and has recently started college, with a major in speech pathology. Beth thanks Trainmate Jack himself for inspiring her poem, as well as her wonderful parents.

Liz Qually graduated from college with a major in political science and economics before giving stand-up comedy a try. She surfs, plays tennis, skateboards and devotes a great deal of time to social causes—from Amnesty International to the East Timor Action Network. Her "Breezy" story was published in *Teen Ink* magazine while she was a junior in high school, and she thanks her English teacher, Ms. Hoogheem, for all of her support.

Heather Quinn graduated from college with a degree in psychology and minor in education. She is pursuing her master's in education and teaching preschool part-time. She loves her students and the ways their little minds work! Heather enjoys reading, hiking and gardening, and continues to write short fiction and poetry. Her piece about overcoming her obsession appeared in *Teen Ink* magazine during her junior year in high school and another piece of hers is featured in *Teen Ink: Our Voices, Our Visions*.

Jorge Quiñones wrote his touching memories of his father his senior year in high school, when it was published in the pages of *Teen Ink* magazine. Now in college, he studies media arts and design and enjoys his favorite hobbies: eating, sleeping and watching sports. Jorge sends a special thank-you to his mom and dad for their continued support.

Vanessa Dawn Rand is a junior in high school. She took this amazing shot of a pile of stones at a local beach. She loves shooting photographs, especially at her family's cabin in the woods. Vanessa loves to snowboard and play the guitar. She plans to major in science in college because she's particularly interested in the study of DNA.

Alice Reagan is currently pursuing an M.F.A. in theater. She is also managing editor for an upcoming issue of the journal, *Women & Performance*. She studied women's literature and theater in college. Her fiction piece, published in *Teen Ink* magazine when she was a high-school senior, has some roots in reality—she worked in a bookstore.

Maritess A. Reusch wrote her very honest piece about supporting her incarcerated brother when she was a sophomore in high school. She is now a journalism major in college and works in a catering business learning to cook. Mari dedicates her work to her parents, who always believed in her and what she could do.

Melanie A. Rice loves to read, write and cook, but nothing brings her more joy than lounging with her cats, Abu and Lex. She thanks her parents for their constant support, and dedicates her work to Carol Crawford, her English teacher, who helped uncover Melanie's true talents. She will be forever grateful and honored. Melanie also thanks the special and dedicated (and often under-appreciated) bus drivers like Ms. Janie about whom she wrote when she was published in *Teen Ink* magazine last year.

Meredith Lee Ritchie keeps her schedule filled with school clubs, tennis, basketball and work (where she met "Superman," the hero of her story) but she loves to hang out with her friends during busy weekends. She recently took an amazing trip to Europe, and can't wait to go again. She thanks her parents, her brother Justin, and the rest of her family and friends for always believing in her. Her piece recently appeared in *Teen Ink* magazine.

Sarah Roberto shot this exuberant photo of her brother in a field last year. A sophomore in high school, she takes primarily landscape photos, so this was an attempt to shoot something with deeper meaning. Sarah plays field hockey and runs winter and spring track at her school. She really enjoys sailing. She would love to be a writer but is keeping all her options open.

Faheem Robinson declares that he loves his life! Through all those years of heartache and pain going from one foster home to another, he didn't realize that these events would actually help mold him into the person he is today. He has more than survived and has become a successful hair stylist! He also realizes he has one of the biggest families because of all his foster homes. His piece was published in *Teen Ink* magazine when he was a senior in high school. He would like to thank everyone who showed him love during his childhood years.

Rachel Roth still enjoys writing, even as a senior in college in the business school, and hopes to incorporate it into her future career, possibly in financial services. She gives campus tours and is quite active in her sorority as well as spending junior year studying in Spain. In high school, Rachel primarily wrote poetry, but ventured into more humorous writing in this essay, which was published in *Teen Ink* magazine when she was a senior. She also kept busy as editor of the foreign-language magazine and captain of the cheerleading team.

Dana Rusk wrote this simple, but perceptive poem as a senior in high school when it was published in *Teen Ink* magazine. She was into sports, participating in field hockey and lacrosse. Although she wrote all through high school, she does little now that she's out of college. At college, she studied environmental science and has been working for two years for an environmental consulting firm.

Michele Sampson brought her love of dance to college; she is working toward a dance minor, and was the winner of a local arts council scholarship for dance. When she's not in toe shoes, she is volunteering as a church teacher and usher, helping the local parks department, fulfilling her duties as the Italian Club president, a board member of National Honor Society and the business manager of her school newspaper. Michele dedicates this piece, written in her junior year, to her biracial niece who, with her innocence and love, inspires Michele to help change the world and stand up to racism.

Barney Schauble has lived and worked in London as a risk manager for a large brokerage firm for a number of years. Recently marrying an English woman, he plans to return to the States soon. The subject of the poem, his brother Oren, is now a junior in high school. When Barney was in high school, he was involved in many activities, including soccer, student politics, academic bowl and drama. He also took and taught karate and spent time with his brothers, parents and friends. Always wanting to travel, he was able to take many trips during his years of living abroad.

Atara Schimmel was a junior in high school when her nostalgic piece appeared in *Teen Ink* magazine. She has since graduated from college in Israel and spent many years doing community service in Africa. She still loves to write.

Emma Schofield, a high-school freshman, actually shot this scene for her very first class assignment. She was taken by the shadow of her two friends created by the sun and so decided to try to capture it. Emma keeps busy playing on the varsity soccer team and loves to ski. Her favorite activity is hanging out with her two older brothers when they come home from college.

Lisa Schottenfeld recently graduated from high school, where she was editor of the newspaper and literary magazine and was involved with chorus and the debate group. She performed in many school theater productions and volunteered as assistant director for her temple's drama club. Her greatest passion is Shakespeare. Published many times in *Teen Ink* magazine, she wrote her portrait of her voice teacher during her senior year and two of her poems appeared in other *Teen Ink* books.

Aaron Schwartz took this amazing close-up of a hand writing as a senior in high school when it appeared in *Teen Ink* magazine. He thought, as he shot it, "Hey, that would be a cool picture." Now, a junior in college, he takes mostly black-and-white portraits and looks to Edward Warner as his favorite photographer. Studying industrial design, he enjoys video games and singing loudly in his car.

Shea M. Seen skipped third grade and graduated the youngest senior in her class. She loves reading, singing, dancing, and above all, acting. In addition to her spirited preface to this book, her childhood wedding tale first appeared in *Teen Ink* magazine a year ago when she was a high-school senior. She dedicates her work to her mom, grandma and "papa," who will always be the "wind beneath her wings."

Sabine Selvais, after getting a college degree in fine arts, became a graphic designer. She is an amazingly creative person, enjoying stained-glass work and decorating, as well as photography. This simple photo of daisies was shot when still in high school and was published in *Teen Ink* magazine. Marrying her long-time boyfriend, she relocated to be closer to her family. She'd like to make a special dedication to her husband since he has given her many opportunities to become a creative person.

Raabia Shafi is just beginning college this year and finds it much harder than high school. She's hoping to double major in history and foreign affairs, but finds she changes her mind a lot. Raabia loves tennis, playing varsity in high school and for pleasure now. Her perceptive piece about her grandmother was published as a senior in high school where she was active in the Islamic Awareness Club. She still loves to write and dedicates this story to her grandmother.

William K. Sheppard created his self-portrait as a senior in high school. Now a college freshman studying business, he plans to pursue his masters in culinary art, physical therapy and music. His long-time dream has been to become a chef and physical therapist. He explains, "I've enjoyed cooking since I was little, and I've always wanted to help people." He also loves music, especially alternative music and jazz. He plays the trombone, drums and steel drums, and is a member of a jazz band and steel pan band. Will says, "Music will be part of my life forever." He thanks his high-school art teachers, Mrs. Skelton and Mrs. Putman.

Selma Siddiqui loves theater, swimming, public speaking and cows ("they're fun, quiet and interesting animals") and she occasionally finds herself singing 1960s songs in the middle of class. Her beautifully crafted portrait of her Pakistani grandfather was published in *Teen Ink* magazine last year when she was a sophomore. She dedicates her piece to Mr. Helms, her English teacher.

Amilcar Silva is following his dream and studies engineering in college. "Sins of the Father" appeared in a recent issue of *Teen Ink* magazine. Amilcar (or AMC, as his friends call him) loves to play football and spends much of his time with his daughter, Shantel, whose birth was his most memorable and moving experience. He thanks his favorite teacher, Ms. Preer, for everything she has done for him.

Ilana Silverman is now a college sophomore thinking about majoring in cognitive science. She wrote her piece in high school where she studied American Sign Language, using her knowledge to be a teaching assistant for a semester at the American School for the Deaf. Ilana loves working with children and continues to volunteer despite her busy college schedule. Ilana dedicates her piece to Deborah Lewison-Grant, her high-school sign-language teacher, who not only taught and inspired her, but also opened a whole new world.

Caty Simon wrote her poem when she was barely in high school where she was quite active in the feminist movement as well as gay rights, participating in many rallies. After high school she became a rape crisis counselor and volunteered at a center. She says that her handwriting hasn't improved since she wrote the poem so many years ago, but she is much nicer to her father!

Stephen Siperstein has had his photographs exhibited in a local arts festival where he also won an essay contest. He is a senior in high school and a musician "to the core." He has been playing the guitar and piano for years, and has even taught children how to play. This summer he will work as a camp counselor. He shoots primarily black-and-white and was a finalist in a national photo contest for *Photographer's Forum Magazine*.

Thomas W. Sitzler recently graduated from high school where he was one well-rounded student: wrestling all four years, singing in the school choir, marching as drum major with the band and receiving the award for Most Spirited Senior (in addition to holding a black belt in karate and being an Eagle Scout)! Now studying choir education in college with an emphasis on piano mirrors his lifelong love of piano and music. On that fateful day senior year when he was handing in this piece on love, a friend grabbed it and insisted he do some editing, polishing it to its present stage as it appeared in *Teen Ink* magazine.

Joanna Sng was published in *Teen Ink* magazine when she was a junior in high school, remembering what it was like to watch her grandmother cook. High school was an amazing time for her, but she says it doesn't even compare to all she's experienced in college. She loves the freedom to be able to meet new people and learn from teachers who have a real interest in helping her grow as a person. Joanne's best adventure was spending a summer working in Disney World in Florida. "It was honestly the most perfect summer ever" where she met her real "Prince Charming."

Linsey A. Stevens wrote her heartfelt tribute to Dr. Mark Boucek a few years ago. Linsey fishes, mountain bikes and backpacks, loves softball and reading, and currently majors in international studies in college. Three open-heart surgeries and numerous hospital stays helped Linsey prioritize her life, and to grow emotionally and spiritually.

Robert M. Stolper wrote this engaging portrait of his teacher when he was a junior in high school. He dedicates it to all the teachers of the world, the second line of parenting who are rarely recognized, and to his family and friends, some of his most important teachers. Rob recently graduated from college with a degree in biochemistry and works for a pharmaceutical consulting company. Since both his parents are teachers, he's spent his summers traveling and has acquired a huge variety of experiences (hiking the Grand Canyon, rock climbing, driving to Alaska and seeing the Northern Lights). He has volunteered for his local ambulance corps since high school.

David J. Stryker wrote his story as a junior in high school, but his love of music described in his piece has followed him to college where he is a regular attendee of New York Philharmonic concerts. He spends several hours a week tutoring children in Hebrew and assisting in the office of a religious school. David has many special acknowledgments: his family for their inspiration and teaching him to persevere, and his friends and community for their support and helping him to see the good in difficult situations.

Joyce Sun believes that her best writing is "spontaneous, quick and comes from the heart," and she proves it—the poem featured here was written in the ten minutes between high-school calculus and French classes when she was a junior. Joyce enjoyed a random set of activities during high school: Quiz Bowl, Youth in Government, helping with theater productions and falling down a lot while trying to play soccer as a freshman. These days she fits in writing between working for her college's classics journal, a law journal on human rights and development, and what she calls "semi-professional" Web design. Joyce is studying biology with the hope of heading to law school after graduation.

Bonnie Tamarin's piece about her mother was originally published in *Teen Ink* magazine when she was a high-school sophomore, where she occasionally wrote for the school paper. She went on to college where she continued to love writing, graduating with a B.S. in Magazine Journalism and a minor in Spanish. Now a social worker (after receiving a Master's this year), she works with the HIV-positive population. Bonnie says she still enjoys writing, although she hasn't written anything for publication since her undergraduate years.

Suzanne Timmons, a senior in high school, is always on the run—she is the team captain for both the indoor and outdoor track teams at her school. When she's not running around the track, she's running around the office of her school newspaper, where she is the editor. In addition, the Key Club, Campus Ministry and the Bridge Over Troubled Waters are all proud to call her a member of their organizations.

Pamela J. Torok feels her camera is her "third eye," her extension and companion for life. For her, the expression, "Don't leave home without it," has taken on new meaning, for she is never without her camera. Graduating from college next year, she is majoring in photography and graphic design. Her lyrical shot of these stone steps was published in *Teen Ink* magazine when she was a junior in high school. She dedicates it to her photography teacher who made every day memorable and to her mom who drove her everywhere so she could take pictures.

Emily N. Trask, now a graduate student and editor for an education research firm, was published in *Teen Ink* magazine as a junior in high school. Her story was inspired by a man she met on a life-changing train trip from Boston to Colorado when she was sixteen years old. She would like to thank "Stiles," wherever he is, as well as Mrs. Lefort, who told her to submit her piece to *Teen Ink*. Lastly, she thanks her family and friends, sending a special message to Matt "for always supporting me, no matter what."

Erica Hillary Trestyn is graduating this year from college with a fine-arts major, continuing her interest in art. This lovely pen-and-ink drawing of a rose was published in *Teen Ink* magazine when Erica was a senior in high school.

Brian Wayne is a senior in high school where he does lots of photography. He also plays guitar in a band and personally recorded a demo track in Nashville when he was only fifteen. He loves tennis, playing for the varsity team at his school, and is involved with the Model UN as well as working as a short-order cook at a restaurant in his town.

Michelle Wedig saw her piece in *Teen Ink* magazine as a senior in high school where she was active in many clubs and sports, including field hockey. She also enjoyed photography, spending lots of time in the darkroom and serving as photo editor for her newspaper. In college, she studied biomedical engineering, and is currently finishing her masters in tissue engineering. She tries to relax by cooking, going to the movies and trying to go to the gym.

Rachel Weiner considers writing a form of meditation since she finds it a way to figure out her deepest, most complicated thoughts and feelings. As a junior in high school, she works two jobs, takes science classes, and is an active member of her school's literary magazine, the Gay-Straight Alliance and Amnesty International. She thanks the subject of her poem for "helping me grow, find out who I am, and trusting me with your heart," and her parents and friends for "always keeping me in your hearts and showing me how to laugh again when I feel like I've forgotten."

Julie White calls herself a beach bum, but she doesn't have much time for laying in the sun. As a senior in high school, she is captain of the soccer team, a basketball cheerleader and a member of the track team. She is the secretary for both her class and her school's National Honor Society, as well as being involved in a peer leader group, SADD, drama, the Student Advisory council and working with children with disabilities. During the summer she has the "awesome" job of being a camp counselor for inner-city kids. Julie would like to thank the staff of *Teen Ink* for their time and effort.

Jon Wright took this panoramic shot of trees when he was in high school. Now working as a landscaper, he is too busy to continue his interest in photography.

Catherine Zimmerman finds nothing more satisfying than incorporating life, imagination and feelings into words on paper. Her moving piece first appeared in *Teen Ink* magazine when she was a senior in high school. Now in college, Catherine plans to major in elementary education. In addition to writing, Catherine has a passion for the martial arts. At age fifteen, she was state champion and is now one rank away from receiving a black belt. Catherine dedicates her piece to the Spargo family and to Mrs. Jeannie Pearson, a wonderful teacher and friend.

"The Kiss." Reprinted by permission of Thomas W. Sitzler. ©2001 Thomas W. Sitzler.

"Learning to Cook." Reprinted by permission of Destie Hohman. ©1997 Destie Hohman.

"His Gift." Reprinted by permission of David Pease. ©2000 David Pease.

"Silhouette of Boy Throwing Ball." Reprinted by permission of Sarah Roberto. ©2002 Sarah Roberto.

"Just One Ride." Reprinted by permission of Rachel Anderson. ©2001 Rachel Anderson.

"Shortcut Home." Reprinted by permission of Cynthia Oquendo. ©2001 Cynthia Oquendo.

"One of a Kind." Reprinted by permission of Brooke Cooper. ©1997 Brooke Cooper.

"Will You Remember Me?" Reprinted by permission of Atara Schimmel. ©1992 Atara Schimmel.

"Girl Sitting on Bench." Reprinted by permission of Alex Marquez. ©1998 Alex Marquez.

"Loving Hands." Reprinted by permission of Beth Bednarz Pruski. ©1992 Beth Bednarz.

"Four Girls Forming Circle." Reprinted by permission of Dyani Jensen. ©1998 Dyani Jensen.

"A Letter to Cupid." Reprinted by permission of Rachel Roth. ©1998 Rachel Roth.

"Don Juan, Goldfish." Reprinted by permission of Lisa Kelly. ©2001 Lisa Kelly.

"Anchor on Beach." Reprinted by permission of Ryan Healy. ©2002 Ryan Healy.

"Calling a Friend." Reprinted by permission of Mallory Ho. ©2001 Mallory Ho.

"Rebels Six." Reprinted by permission of Christopher Gubelmann. ©2001 Christopher Gubelmann.

"Person Hanging on Window." Reprinted by permission of Patrick Michael Baird. ©2000 Patrick Michael Baird.

"The Date." Reprinted by permission of Sierra Black. ©1996 Sierra Frank.

"Trainmate Jack." Reprinted by permission of Beth M. Putnam. ©1997 Beth M. Putnam.

"Stiles." Reprinted by permission of Emily N. Trask. ©1993 Emily N. Trask.

"Pile of Rocks." Reprinted by permission of Vanessa Dawn Rand. ©2001 Vanessa Dawn Rand.

"Fallen Rock Zone." Reprinted by permission of Farrah Lehman. ©2000 Farrah Lehman.

Get Them All!

"As a parent and storyteller, I find great hope for the future based on the depth of feeling and creativity in this unique book."
George Lucas, filmmaker

Teen Ink
Our Voices, Our Visions

Written by Teens

Sharing Thoughts On:
Friends
Fitting In
Love
Challenges
Family
Heroes
Loss
Memories

Edited By
Stephanie H. Meyer
and John Meyer

Code #8164 • Paperback • $12.95

Each *Teen Ink* book captures the essence of what it means to be a teenager by offering a diverse collection of prose, poetry, fiction and art all representing the moments that help to define teen life.

Teen Ink
More Voices, More Visions

Written by Teens

Speaking Out On:
Love
Friends
Challenges
Family
Memories
Fitting In
Milestones

Edited By
Stephanie H. Meyer
and John Meyer

Code #9136 • Paperback • $12.95

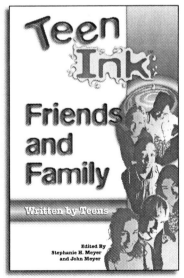

Teen Ink
Friends and Family

Written by Teens

Edited By
Stephanie H. Meyer
and John Meyer

Code #9314 • Paperback • $12.95

To order direct: Telephone (800) 441-5569 • www.hcibooks.com
Prices do not include shipping and handling. Your response code is BKS.

Printed in the United States
132208LV00003B/2/A